The Truth Game

ALSO BY VANESSA NICOLSON

The Sculpture of Maurice Lambert

Have You Been Good?

In memory of my father,
Benedict Nicolson (1914–1978)

All truth needs is to be seen and heard.
It will look after itself after that.

KEITH VAUGHAN,
JOURNAL 14 JULY 1958[1]

CONTENTS

Envy's Ear 1

1 Infatuation

Daughter 7
Father 11
Julie 30
Mr Right 46

2 Faith

Malú 63
Pat 78
Lydia 94
Steve 110
Mary 127

3 Frailty

Vanessa 141
Em & Jean 155
Adam 175
Luisa 193
Ben 206

Coda 213

Acknowledgements 217
Notes 218
List of Illustrations 219

Inconstancy, *Wrath* and *Envy* by Giotto

ENVY'S EAR

A ROW OF DOOMED FIGURES ARE TORTURED AND CONSUMED by human weakness. *Inconstancy* whirls unsteadily on a rolling disc, unbalanced and mid-fall on a sloping floor; *Wrath* arches her back as she tears at her clothes in fury, revealing her chest; *Envy*'s serpent tongue lashes her with her own malicious spite; *Desperation* is hung by despair as a fiend arrives to claim her soul. Meanwhile *Folly*, the large-bellied jester, strikes a pose, and *Infidelity,* bound by a lead around his neck to the female figure he holds in the palm of his hand, appears trapped by his own temptation.

Justice and *Injustice* face each other across the chapel. Both are enthroned rulers: *Justice* a beautiful queen with scales in hand, denoting fairness and equality for her subjects, *Injustice* a cruel king gripping the hilt of a sword. Like the other vices he does not see, for in the visual language of the time he is blind to righteousness and truth.

The Arena Chapel in Padua is described by the guidebooks as an early-fourteenth-century 'jewel'. My mother took me there as a child in the 1960s when the place was empty of tourists, and began telling me the stories that Giotto had depicted in bands along the walls: the *Life of the Virgin* and the *Life of Christ*. She never noticed that my head was not moving along the rows of framed vignettes in time with her narrative. This was because my eyes were transfixed by the images in grisaille on the faux-marble dados below:

the *Seven Deadly Sins* or *Vices*, given a human face. These hapless creatures, destroyed by their own imperfections, seemed to me so much more compelling than the stable, composed serenity of the *Virtues* on the opposite wall, or the Bible stories running above. To my childish eyes they appeared like characters from a fairy story. They were witches or wizards steeped in darkness, up to no good.

I returned to that chapel as an adult and bought myself a postcard of *Invidia* (*Envy*), seen with her attributes: the oversized ear to listen to malevolent gossip, the snake to spread snide words, the sack of money held closely and unshared. The fire licking her dress inflames the jealousy that consumes her.

'The serpent hissing between the lips of *Envy* is so huge, it fills her wide-open mouth so completely, that the muscles of her face are strained and contorted, like that of a child swelling a balloon with its breath,' wrote Marcel Proust in *À la recherche du temps perdu*.

Envy sat on my desk as I wrote about my life, after my nineteen-year-old daughter Rosa died. The serpent mirrored my own fate. My mouth was so full of bitterness and pain that I too felt there was not enough space to contain it all. It made me think of the other allegories that give human form to troublesome feelings. Like *Inconstancy*, many times I quivered untethered on unstable ground, envious of others' secure bases, jealous of their healthy children, blinded by my own despair. Giotto's images still resonate with me, for they tell of feelings we try to keep hidden and held down: the mad, the uncontainable, the things thought best unspoken.

But envy in particular intrigues me. So often the object or situation or person that is envied has little in common with the fantasy created around it. As well as writing about loss, I had tried to shed light on the dark side of a childhood people generally view as 'privileged'.[2] I have lost count of the number of times a mention of my upbringing in Florence or holidays with my cousins in a castle in Kent is met with wistful longing. 'Oh, how exotic to have grown up in Florence,' people say, 'How wonderful to have holidayed at Sissinghurst.' Yes, so it would seem, and of course in many respects it *was* all extremely privileged. But they do not hear when I go on to say that it was lonely and unstable, that this had repercussions. This is not the line they want delivered.

I am guilty of the reverse. I romanticise what I perceive are the 'ordinary' families I see around me, with their network of nurture and support. I convince myself that everything would have been fine 'if only' I had had siblings and devoted, available parents. But of course that is not necessarily a guarantee to a stable life.

When I was young, my father and I played a 'truth game'. But there was much we did not learn, for behind the apparent honesty of our answers we had wider histories that we failed to disclose. It is this that interests me. After writing my memoir I began thinking more about the stories we do not know, the 'back stories' of people who intersect with our own lives. There was still so much I had not discovered about those whose paths have crossed mine, even characters I thought I knew well.

These are the stories I wish to excavate. As far as possible I have asked their permission to explore how in our different ways we navigate life and relationships, and what you learn if you go back to those you are – or have been – close to, and discuss things in a way you never normally would, as so much is usually left unsaid, and so much is unknown.

My mother never talked about my father's departure from their marriage, or the death of her mother or that of her granddaughter. She has her own version of events and a tendency to blame. Her view is: she was abandoned by a selfish and irresponsible husband; a few years later her mother received the wrong medical treatment and would otherwise have been saved; her granddaughter Rosa's early death was a blessing for in later life she would have struggled with her epilepsy and been hurt by an uncaring world that did not understand it. We were mismatched and disconnected that way, for I always longed for explanations and conversations whereas my mother decided what the 'truth' was and saw no point in delving further.

I know people will interpret as they wish, and (like *Envy*'s ear) will not always be receptive to the whole truth. And clearly it is sometimes necessary to keep secrets or respect the secrets of others. A handful of times in this book I have had to conceal facts or disguise identities to protect my subjects from possible repercussions. Generally however, I believe in getting to the heart of things, 'the very stuff of life,' as the writer Graham Swift has said.[3] For if conversations can be had, and truths unravelled and revealed, perhaps misunderstandings, resentments and most of all that insidious emotion – shame – may be put to rest.

I

INFATUATION

Daughter

It is early August, over four decades ago, and the train carriage is hot. Opposite the girl sits her father, fifty-seven years old, balding and thin, sweaty and red faced, sporting the short-sleeved, checked shirt and crumpled summer trousers he always chose to pack when going abroad. She is almost sixteen and is wearing blue cotton loons and a white cheesecloth smock. Her limbs are long and her lean face divided by curtains of black hair. The bag lying beside her on the brown leatherette seat is made of heavy cloth and rope handles, and embroidered with a picture of an urn. Inside it is a half-eaten baguette she began before they left Paris. That, a Coca-Cola bottle, and a packet of cigarettes – to smoke in the corridor while her father pretends not to see – is all she will need for the journey.

They are sitting facing each other by the window, and they are alone. Her father has done his trick of coughing profusely every time anyone looks as if they are considering coming into the carriage. This almost always results in making passengers change their mind about joining them. They hesitate, looking momentarily unsettled, then move further along. Her father does not try this if the train is very crowded, but it usually works to keep boorish-looking gentlemen and grumpy old women away. His second strategy is to become 'a madman' (his words), again to put passengers off so that they might have the carriage to themselves. Whenever someone appears at the door, he begins rolling his eyes and pretending with his hands to climb up an imaginary wall. This used to amuse but now only succeeds in embarrassing the girl. She blushes and pleads with him to stop. Later in life she would find such behaviour unconscionable.

The coughing isn't so bad. She can cope with the coughing. He does that anyway as he smokes so many cigarettes. Even more than she does.

Her father loves games, and they had always played them together. When she was very little it was Grandfather's Footsteps. He would stand by a tree in Hyde Park or at the end of the long paths framed by hedges at his parents' home, turn his back to her and wait. She would make her way towards him from far away, creeping up as silently as possible, but then his sudden turns would catch her moving, and she would run giggling back to the beginning. When she was a bit older, say seven or eight, he sat her down and announced that he was going to teach her how to play chess. Much to his disappointment, she never had the patience to understand the rules. Later it was her turn to introduce him to the card games she had learnt at school, and more recently her favoured board games like Mastermind, where he has to guess which sequence of four coloured pegs she has hidden behind a plastic cover.

But their favourite has always been the Truth Game. It involves taking turns to ask each other a question. The only rule is that the replies have to be honest and truthful.

'What was the most embarrassing moment you have ever had?'

'Have you ever lied to your best friend?'

'If you had to choose between ice cream or chocolate cake which would it be?'

'Would you tell the truth if the truth were hurtful?'

Often, their answers would prompt discussions, as the questioner interjected, agreeing or disagreeing, asking further questions that the original had prompted, and so on. Occasionally a stranger who had not been put off coming into the carriage or was sitting next to them in a restaurant would want to join in, amused by their father-daughter conversations. 'I couldn't help overhearing…'

The train is rushing through the French countryside. They left Paris a couple of hours ago and are becoming restless. The carriage window is impossible to open. It is so hot. The girl kicks off her espadrilles and stretches her long legs diagonally across to the seat next to her father. She has almost finished *The Magus* and wants to save the end of the book for later. Her father has been reading a biography of a politician that to her eyes looks really boring. They won't be in the south of France for ages.

'Daddy, let's play the Truth Game!' she says.

Her father looks up and smiles as he marks the page he has reached with a postcard and closes the book.

'You begin.'

She had met up with her father in Paris, having taken the overnight train from Italy. It was strange to be going back towards that same country again a few days later, but the stopover in Paris had been an opportunity for her father to see some art exhibitions – dragging her along, for her interest in art is not yet acknowledged, even to herself – and for them to spend time together before travelling south to stay with his painter friend Rodrigo. Over meals in Parisian bistros she had moaned about the miserable time she had spent with her strict Italian mother in Florence. Her mother was the opposite of this liberal, unconventional father – one reason why they had divorced a decade earlier.

The girl tells her father that the repercussions of her mother reading her diary the previous summer are still being acted out. She doesn't trust me, she gives me no freedom, she treats me like a child, and so on.

'She is always angry about something. Why can't she be a modern, enlightened mother who allows me to be myself? After all it's 1972, not 1872!'

Never once does her father criticise her mother. He always presents her point of view.

'She worries about you. She minds because she cares.'

Perhaps it is because that conversation is still fresh or perhaps it is because she is missing a boy from school, but as the train rattles remorselessly on, the first question she formulates for the Truth Game is this: 'Apart from with Mummy, have you ever been so in love that you would have liked to marry someone else?'

For a second, she is struck by the sad expression crossing her father's face. She will remember this.

He is hesitant in his reply. 'Yes, I have been in love, apart from with your mother. But I couldn't marry them.'

The daughter is excited by this revelation. 'Who? Who? Was she married already?' she asks playfully.

'That wasn't the reason.'

'Was she in love with someone else then?' She is grinning.

'That would be telling,' he answers, raising his bushy eyebrows.

'Oh go on!' she pleads, enjoying the game. 'Do I know her?'

'No, that's enough.' He smiles. 'It's my turn to ask a question now. Let me see... hmm... I've got one. Do you feel more English or Italian?'

Father

She remembers the black-and-white photograph taken in the late 1940s. A striking young man standing in St Mark's Square in Venice, arm outstretched, feeding the pigeons. He is smiling, Hollywood-matinee-idol-handsome, in baggy trousers, casual jacket and brogues, framed by the birds swooping down to eat out of his hands.

The image had been blown up to a size perfect for a large silver frame (or perhaps an Italian leather one), to sit on a side table, or desk, or prominent shelf. But it was never displayed. She found it among her father's papers, soon after he had died, and she wishes now she had not mislaid it so she could see it again. She wishes too that she could remember at what point she read the account of her father's love for this man in the journal he left – because she only met the fabled David once, many years later, and disliked him instantly. Was that because she knew how much her father had suffered over the affair, or because the man treated her, a bereaved young woman of only twenty-one years, with such supercilious sarcasm?

Like the Venetian pigeons, people would also eat out of David's hands. His reputation for brilliance as an art connoisseur travelled wide. 'Unknown' masterpieces were uncovered and rescued by David from corners of attics and stables and embassies and homes (both modest and stately), or bought for a fraction of their market value at auction, and then re-attributed by his expert eye. Some of these priceless works of art – *The Musicians* by Caravaggio, a group of decorative paintings by Tiepolo, *Psyche showing her Sisters her Gifts from Cupid* by Fragonard – now grace the walls of famous collections such as the Metropolitan Museum in New York and the National Gallery in London. His instincts were razor sharp and his expertise prodigious, but he lacked the patience to sit down and consign his thoughts to paper. Consequently he did not publish, so never established any lasting authority as a scholar.

Her father and David began their affair while the latter was still a student at Oxford. In 1948, when the journal entries were written, David was twenty-one and her father Ben thirty-four. Ben had become editor of an academic art-history magazine the year before. Earlier that summer they had made a trip together to Italy, where Ben had introduced David to the eminent art historian Bernard Berenson and they had visited many other private and public collections. By the time they returned to London, Ben was besotted – and deluded himself that his feelings were reciprocated.

Ben died in May 1978, and his daughter, still a student, was heart-broken. A short while later David, who had become an art dealer, dedicated a small exhibition on Georges Seurat to the memory of his ex-lover. Ben had owned a small sketch by the artist (which he bequeathed to a friend) and Seurat was also the subject of the first book he had planned but never published.

There was a smart dinner given after the private view to which the girl and her mother were invited. David fixed her with an amused glint in his eye as she was introduced.

'Oh, this is the daughter! Isn't *that* extraordinary,' he sniggered, giving the word 'that' an emphasis she didn't like, as he turned to another smirking Jermyn Street art dealer on his right.

She watched him all evening. She observed quietly, resentfully, taking note of everything. David took the floor like a performer, mimicking, gossiping and amusing his audience. There was an edge of cruelty to his wit that she found disconcerting. When, finally, her mother voiced their thanks and goodbyes on behalf of them both, he murmured as he took the daughter's hand, 'you've looked rather sullen all evening, have you not enjoyed yourself?' He did not say it in a kind, conciliatory way, but harshly, like an accusation.

'Oh no, I mean yes, that is, absolutely...' she stammered and, flushing, clumsily dropped the catalogue she had been holding on to the floor, to which he chuckled, addressing the assembled guests, 'My goodness isn't she so like her father!'

She walked out of the gallery door angry and upset, disconcerted by the sound of the male laughter behind her.

Three years later she heard he had died of cancer, aged fifty-five.

Saturday 14 August 1948

Since David got back from Ireland a week ago, we have been wrapped up in each other to the exclusion of everything else.

I think that 10 days separation has done the world of good to both of us: we have grasped (he has grasped at last) that we cannot do without each other – not so much that it is agreeable to meet every night, but that it is necessary to do so. And I have never known D. so gentle and affectionate – he has recognised my distaste for pansiness, for too many jokes about guardsmen, eyeing people in the street etc., and he has refrained from doing so – in fact he has become altogether more serious, loving, nursing our relationship. He has not been out for pleasure this week. Pleasure now comes to us incidentally, without any apparent effort; I think we are both satisfied merely to be in each other's company; the circumstances of our meetings have now taken second place. I think he is in love with me. But he does not tell me so, for fear I believe that if he should say truthfully 'yes, I am', I might become elated and later dejected or utterly miserable if he fell out of love again. (I see that David does not trust himself to remain constant, he is ashamed of his inconstancy and is determined that I should not get a taste for it, as it might end by destroying my love for him, which he holds dear.) And I do not ask him whether it is true, in case he should be forced to say that it is not, and we should find ourselves back where we started in April. So the crucial fact remains unexplored, hovering between us. I do not need to mind very much whether it is or not, since I am confident of his devotion – and if his devotion can grow slowly, unforced, into love and passion, then there will be a chance of passion lasting. I am not anxious to persuade him of things that cannot be true.

I slept with him every night from Saturday to Wednesday – the weekend at 'S.' and later at Neville Terrace where he lived with me. I shall never forget the perfect harmony of our lives at Neville Terrace, having breakfast every morning together in dressing gowns, only speaking when we had something we wished to say, otherwise remaining just as happily silent, I never losing consciousness of him beside me. It has taught me how by nature I am smugly domestic, bourgeois, loving peace and amicable relationships and compatible living. And he is most beautiful of all at breakfast before he has brushed his hair, I would have to rise from my chair periodically to cover him with kisses, I could not let ten minutes pass without expressing my feelings. I feel I could go for ever lying with him in bed, then leaving him to sleep in the early hours, and returning to his bed in the early morning to kiss his soft, silky hair as it lies tousled on the pillow, and watch him as he wakes up becoming slowly conscious of my presence, slowly putting his arms around my neck. No experience that I have ever had can compare with the beauty of these moments. And never a sense of doing wrong, of saucy wickedness, but only the conviction that it is right and necessary for both of us, that we both become altogether nicer, fuller, richer human beings for the experience. In fact, I now realise that I was only half a human

> being without it. And all those years I wasted! It seems that I was just waiting for him to grow up, waiting for the time when he was old enough to love me.[4]

There were five rooms in the flat her father had lived in since he and her mother divorced. Some provided more than one function: apart from Ben's bedroom, bathroom and kitchen, the sitting room doubled up as Ben's study and the spare bedroom was also the library and dining room. It had a single bed placed alongside one of the floor to ceiling bookcases that covered the walls and this is where she would sleep when staying with him during holidays from school or later, university.

Sometimes, before turning off the light she would reach out her hand, pull out one of the books, and browse. The section by the bed was more randomly organised than in the rest of the room, where artists and periods were grouped together for easy access. Here there were books on photography, art from Africa and India and ancient Greece, a selection of literary magazines and a row of clothbound journals dating from the 1930s through to the 1950s. She laughed at the *Young Physique* magazines and the *National Geographic* placed next to the photography catalogues, which featured images of beautiful naked youths perched in trees or other natural settings. It never crossed her mind to wonder why her father had them. She may have simply thought, 'my father is an art historian and he admires the beauty of the male form'.

Nosily, she had checked out the journals. But her father's handwriting was so tiny and hard to read, and what she read was not always of interest to a teenager, involving as it did accounts of museums visited and paintings seen or his opinions on people encountered, most of whom she had never heard of.

Just occasionally her attention would be drawn to something more personal. A sentence about returning drunk from a party, or some inadequacy expressed, and then she would perk up, for it was engaging and human and made her father seem more real. These confessions were so much easier to relate to than musings over the merits of Seurat over Signac, even if she *was* studying art history. She wanted to know what people were really thinking and feeling, especially him, and although she adored her father he could be distant, silent, inscrutable. The expression 'a closed book' seemed invented for him. His friends would laugh that no one ever knew if he was going to finish his favourite phrase, 'It was *absolutely...*' with 'marvellous' or 'ghastly'.

It is only now that she wonders why he left those journals so near the bed she occupied, in her line of vision. Was he unconsciously putting things her way in order for her to discover and penetrate his true character? Or was it safer for him to edit facts into the Truth Game?

> I do not think I could have loved anyone else to the same extent. Because during the course of these years I have gradually formulated to myself the vision of the perfect lover. D. is the only person I have ever met who has compared to that vision – not perhaps the D. of April, the smart Oxford undergraduate, out for pleasure and excitement, prepared to sacrifice anything for a moment's titillation, but the D. of August, grown up (David has grown into a man in three months) with obligations and responsibilities, beginning to realise that he knows nothing, that he has everything to learn and that it is all worth learning, that I am the person who can teach him – although I know nothing about Rembrandt and make spoonerisms and dry up in conversation and am not witty, and not very young and have a thirties background of blind left-wing prejudices. One of the most encouraging facts about our love affair is my conviction, unshakeable, that I am doing D. a great deal of good and no harm (a conviction that

> his parents, all lawyers, and the whole world except our friends could never share).
>
> David is more loving than he has ever been. He used only to express his feelings in bed or when drunk. Now he seizes every opportunity to make some endearing remark to me – even in the street he may take my hand suddenly if he feels nobody is looking – and we always whisper affectionate goodbyes even in public, in railway stations. This is partly to be explained by his warmer feelings towards me, but partly also because he has become braver, more forthcoming as the months have passed – and this goes for me too, who used to be faintly embarrassed by love making, owing to inexperience, uncertainty where exactly I stood, terrified always of a minor rebuff or reproof, and fear of being exposed by hostile, inquisitive passers-by. Also we do not now take such care to keep the fact of our love affair from friends, and everyone knows, more people probably than either of us suppose. I do not think any harm can come from this, since no one who knows us is likely to pass on the information to anyone who would wish to do us harm.

How exhausting to maintain that constant vigilance. It beggars belief that homosexuals were once stigmatised as 'deviates', that homosexuality was so condemned that it was considered a mental disorder requiring brutal treatment. At the time Ben was writing, criminal proceedings remained a real threat. During the war it seems there was more of a 'turning a blind eye' attitude, but during the late 1940s and 1950s prosecutions increased, and the police generated genuine fear. This is well-documented territory but no less shocking for that.

At least Ben felt able to be truthful to both his parents, who – in their unconventional marriage – indulged in affairs with their own gender. 'My darling Mummy,' he wrote in May 1948, 'I write this, instead of saying it all, [how typical!] partly because I have had no opportunity during the last twenty-four hours, partly because it is less embarrassing so. I will give you the facts as baldly as possible. I have fallen desperately in love with the young man you may have heard Daddy mention as he met him... an undergraduate at Christ Church... It is much the most overwhelming experience I have ever had, and ever expect to have again. They say these things are wicked, they put you in prison for it: but this experience has brought out in me qualities (kindness, generosity, consideration for others) that I never believed I possessed.'

But even his bohemian parents were concerned that their son's infatuation might lead to a 'scandal' and end in disgrace. 'He is bound to fall out with D. again... and there he would be stranded, having lost his career for the sake of a clever little boy who is not worth the sacrifice,' his mother wrote to his father, followed by, 'How I wish, that he, of all people, could marry and have children... It is all a great pity, and really my heart aches for him sometimes.'

8 October 1948

> D. is not in love with me. He told me so yesterday in Onslow Gardens, when drunk. He is perfectly truthful when drunk. On the other hand, he says he derived from our Italian journey more happiness than he has ever previously known; and that he feels for me more affection than for any of his friends, all the affection of which he is capable. This is not a great deal, but it will increase, I understand him better week by week. His failure to love more, be more natural, be more composed, be at his ease when something more than chatter or gossip is demanded of him, must be blamed on his idiotic parents, against whose standards of morality he has rebelled all his life, and inevitably rebelled wrongly, e.g. instead of allowing himself to love in defiance of them he indulges in

every promiscuous intrigue in defiance of them. Instead of having acquired a different, more enlightened code of morality, he has lost all sense of morality, neither praises nor blames anybody (because they praise and blame everybody), finds sympathetic explanations for their behaviour (because they refuse to admit that decent people can behave in decent ways). Result: ceaseless, pointless pursuit of pleasure. To seduce soldiers in trains is to D. like picking some succulent iris and arranging it in a vase, mere aesthetic dabbling. Hence he must dabble in art and music, and probe into nothing.

This at any rate was the situation until I came along – I, solid, austere, puritanical, older, in a position to help him materially. At first he sees the practical advantage of courting my acquaintance. Then, my composure begins to affect him, he sees in me an anchor, his chief hope of stability, and happiness. My role: to advance an alternative pattern of behaviour to that his parents have to offer. It will consist of: recommendations to work hard (to study Andrea del Sarto); to give up soldiers; to pick friends more carefully; generally not to fritter time away; to avoid smartness, society; to be loyal to intimate friends; to be truthful to love. I tell him that if he does not love he will only be half a person. It may seem from this that I have two ends in view: one, to separate him from his parents; two, to force him to fall in love with me. And of course I should like both these things to happen. Probably I shall succeed in both but he will fall in love with someone else. I shall have achieved my aim, but it will be the death of me. I feel now that were I to lose him, I should have nothing more to hope from life.

There was that terrible occasion in Bond Street once when I fell out of love with him for twenty minutes. It was as though the whole life had been pumped out of me. I thought that this must be an experience that nobody but I had ever had, or at least ever noticed, and recorded. Then on reading Stendhal's *De l'Amour*, I came on the same experience described. Reading this book when in love is like seeing the reflection of one's character in a magic mirror.

This evening Keith Eccleston advanced the theory that D. was always getting waylaid by soldiers, one never knew what had become of him. He drew a picture of a wayward, sensuous youth, utterly unreliable, with an unquenchable thirst for cheap pleasure. I said that in Italy I had never found this so, that always he had followed me around like a gentle, entrancing dog. Perhaps said K.E., he had some respect for your age. For some reason this terrible conversation did not depress me, because I suppose I was certain that K.E.'s explanation was totally inadequate, that D. is passionately devoted to me, that his faithfulness was due to more than mere kindness, more than just a wish to spare me pain. This question of faithfulness is still one that is unresolved between us.

If he goes to Italy next year, I can hardly demand of him that he remain loyal to me, not with the habits of promiscuity that he has formed, not for a whole year. Instead I shall demand that he describe in detail every sexual experience that he has – then it will seem to him and me like picking flowers, then I shall not be tortured by uncertainty. The other night he chucked a dinner engagement with me to dine with his father; and when I persuaded him to meet before dinner, he arrived almost an hour late. This was made up for by his telling me on our next meeting that he had suffered from my moroseness. We have been talking vaguely these last weeks about sharing a house together: and I am glad to say he refers to this constantly as though it were settled: such words as 'that would look nice in our flat', pointing to a Le Nain.

I give him presents constantly. I am going to try and bring him a present every time I see him. How he does respond to my admonitions! He is never pansy with me now, he has discovered exactly how

> I like him to behave, he always behaves sensibly, unostentatiously now – so different from 6 weeks ago. I am much gratified when his friends comment on the fact.

Over the years people occasionally asked, 'when did you discover that your father was homosexual and what did it mean to you?'

His daughter cannot answer for she does not know. Does it matter? From a very early age she was aware of her family being configured differently and of her father being unlike other dads. For a start her parents were separated and she had no siblings. They were not a unit. But was there a moment of revelation when she realised and everything fell into place?

No there was not.

However, she learnt more about her father through this journal than from anywhere or anyone else. It gave her insights into his personality and the inevitability of failure in her parents' marriage. That failure wasn't just about his homosexuality. It was about a romanticism that could never be lived up to, it was about recklessness and withdrawal, self-destruction and guilt, self-awareness and delusion and the need for sociability and solitude. She identifies with these extremes and contradictions of character and sees them reflected in the relationships she has had, both with others and herself.

14 October 1948

> I wish I could describe accurately my feelings. I have not enough skill for this, I can only make it sound boring and egotistical. What shall I say that is true? That only the hours spent in his company have any meaning for me, all the other hours are waiting for the next time. (Nothing but trite sentiments, but how does one make love not trite, not school-girlish? Love is not a subject for literature any more, one either has to describe love and jealousy, or love and

politics, or love and vice to be interesting or keep quiet and suffer platitudinously.)

I experienced suffering on Sunday last. The usual story: I return with him to my hotel, he disappears at the door, I rush up to my room to wait for him, he doesn't come, next morning he has a perfectly adequate explanation of non-appearance. All unimportant, but temporarily it throws me into the depth of despair. I lie in bed panting for serenity of mind. I suffer too much from trivial acts of neglect – which turn out not to be neglect at all – it is only that he consumes my whole being, and unreasonably I demand that I should consume the whole of his. Unreasonably since he does not love me. This is all terrifying because it shows how much I should suffer were anything seriously to go wrong. He gives me all the affection of which he is capable – but for my liking this is insufficient. I want him, as I told him, to become part of my soul. 'If you let me become part of you,' I wrote to him, 'I can be your salvation in life, if not your heart will wither.'

I remember lying on Monday morning on top of him on my bed, listening to his heartbeats, and not being able to hear them (either through deafness or listening to the wrong side) and suddenly saying, 'have you a heart?'

I sometimes wonder when people fall in love whether they are consumed to the same extent as I am. I cannot believe that to them everything else seems so commonplace, even things that should be important, like heavenly evenings spent with friends with drink flowing – oh! I have been to dozens of parties that I have not bothered to mention here because D. was not present.

25 October 1948

It is all up. Last Friday was the day of crisis. D. met me at the train. He had had his hair cut too short, looked hideous, his nose was red: this emboldened me to criticise him too freely, to upbraid him for pansy gestures, to speak unnecessarily harshly about his friends – and then in his room afterwards to seize his copy of Fischel's *Raphael* and fling it on the floor – the copy I had bought him – and force him into intimacy. I could not bear at that moment a discussion about Raphael's drawings. So I began plying him with questions: why couldn't he love me? What was wrong with me? What made him so indifferent, off-hand these last weeks? Why did he treat me so casually? And it all came out, all these things he had really told me before but I had never heeded, never dared face up to. He loved tough, brutal people 3 years older than himself of great beauty. He spoke more truthfully than ever before – or so I had the impression, perhaps it was merely that I listened more carefully. In any case, I realised at last that he could never love me. And I realised that what had sustained me all these months was the hope that one day he would capitulate, that all the love and tenderness and passion and gifts I had bestowed on him week by week would end by softening him. It has made him hard. He was harder this night than I have ever known him – little firm, undeviating eyes looking out at me as the truth passed his lips. But I could see it was an effort, a prodigious effort, and he twisted my hair in knots the whole time, forcing the words out, and I caressing his chest. I do not think we could have kept up this artificiality much longer, I was growing maddened by the static quality of our friendship, never improving, always puzzling and precarious.

I suppose I assumed the explanation would never be as harsh as it turned out to be – I could not have expected such harsh words from him after the last letter I received from him, from Paris, when he said our friendship was the most important of his life, that he gave me all the affection of which he was capable, etc. I expected that if I heard the truth, there would be some hope for the future but he gave me nothing. Then I asked him a final question, whether he enjoyed or positively disliked my sleeping with him, and he said, sometimes one thing, sometimes the other, that he realised he had to if our association was to continue.

Then I behaved badly. I said, well if you don't find it too bad, you must come to bed with me now – and I insisted on his standing naked before me so that I could admire – a thing he hates doing – that combined with sexual relations on top of an emotional crisis, that I know he loathes after a similar experience in Venice – all this was sadistic on my part and it took me a long time to rouse him at all, but then I did not mind because I was in a fever of lust for him and I love his body when it is limp, unaroused. Poor darling, I was ruthless, determined, unkind. This is what love and frenzy makes a kind, easy-going, sensitive person like myself into. And all the time D. remaining so calm and patient, perhaps it was his good temper that aroused me, infuriated me. But we parted friends.

Next morning I visited him again and we had a terrible scene in the kitchen. I told him he had not talent for intimacy, that he was inhuman, unreal, that his upbringing had made him secretive, not a person at all, that all his gaiety and flashiness was a shield for the poverty of his inner life – oh dear! I must have said some terrible things but the words came pouring out, there was nothing to stop them, and D. sat silently listening. I had begun this interview only to tell D. that I could not come down to Oxford for at least a month. But as I went on speaking, despair overwhelmed me, there seemed that there was nothing left of magic between us, nothing at all, that there was nothing to be gained except misery by my continuing to see him. So I said: 'am leaving you now' and I put on my overcoat and stumbled to the door, not daring to look at him – and when he rose from his chair and rushed to me, I left the room and would not let him follow me.

I now do courage tests with memory. I begin by recalling all the episodes during the past eight months when D. has behaved inadequately. This is easy. Then the episodes in which he has come off adequately – more difficult. I hope in this way to end recalling our happiest moments without sorrow. And the last stage of all: the rereading of his letters without a tear; true love will be dead. The photograph of him on my mantelpiece, feeding pigeons in the piazza, I did not dare look at it, I had to grope for it with my eyes shut and shove it in a drawer and I cannot bring myself to reread the earlier pages of this diary. That is why tonight (25th) I had to begin a new page.

30 October 1948

I am afraid there is nothing for it, it is all over. We shall now be hopelessly self-conscious in each other's presence – I in my determination not to show the affection that will be embarrassing to him, will become cold and artificial. He, equally determined not to be subjected to intimacy, will become defiant, more pansy, even smarter, more intolerable than ever. And we cannot, as I thought we might, R. put me right on this, we cannot go on existing on a superficial level, because even that level will be different, more artificial than the same level was before – the relationship between people being an organic thing that is easily upset at whatever level one likes to behave at. We cannot even say, 'right, we will give up that and that and make do with that and that' because all that will happen is that our conversation and behaviour will become phonier and phonier. So I shall just break with him, and trust that I have the strength not to see him, not to try and communicate with him again.

But I go on the same as ever: take my bus, read my *Statesman*, smoke my cigarettes, make conversation at the Beefsteak – just as the body is able to survive all the buffetings of weather, poison, disease, so the soul finds relief from torture in routine, work, friends, drink.

That's exactly how it is, she thought, her teenage mind comparing her recently broken heart with that of her own father's twenty-five years before. Of course this makes her laugh now, oh the arrogance of youth in comparing herself to a sophisticated, adult man. Her father writes so beautifully about love – its pain, obsession and joy – as if setting a standard to be attained, maybe even to be envied. But she wasn't so wrong. The pain of rejection was as raw, the search for oblivion and release just as real. She had written to her father once from boarding school before she read his words in the journal, telling him she was miserable and lost. He had responded by advising her to read, to paint, to find some activity to engage and distract her. She was angry and upset that he seemed to confuse misery with boredom. She was not a child, she felt, to be diverted with new toys, her pain was real and deep and he was not taking it seriously. But later she realised that his lack of patience was understandable. He recognised that vulnerability in himself, the susceptibility to abject despondency, and knew it had to be fought and conquered at all costs.

1 October 1949

I have been in Paris and Venice – golden days. I had dreaded my visit, thinking that every moment I would be haunted by the ghost of David, in the piazza, in the *Flore*, in the wagon-lit with someone else in the bed above me – not being able to wake up in the morning, climb to the upper bunk and kiss him and flatten his hair on the pillow – but it turned out quite differently. How odd, the way one can never plan for pleasure, avoid misery, but can only wait and see what happens. I scarcely thought about him the whole time. I was too busy in the Bellini and Gauguin exhibitions, frantically scribbling notes in my catalogue, I scarcely had a meal alone, I met friends everywhere, delightful, unexpected people, as pleased to

> see me as I to see them – and whenever some empty hour loomed ahead, it was unexpectedly and agreeably filled. Divine evenings, sitting out in the Colombo, eating calamaletti [sic] with the Becketts, Luisa Vertova and a charming young man called John White. And the beauty of the Venetian boys skipping about in their short shorts and long legs. I had none of the *Death in Venice* sensations that I dreaded. It was all so gay and uncorrupt.

The young Italian art historian, then twenty-eight, with whom he ate calamaretti outside the Colombo in Venice in warm autumn sunshine, was certainly an attractive and delightful young woman. But most of all she was clever and knowledgeable, with a quickness of mind and an independence of thought, like him; so different from the vacuous debutantes he met at London parties, 'with their eager smiles and opening remarks and idiotic little conversations and their stupidity and lack of imagination,' as he had described them to an old friend. When this reserved English gentleman asked if he could correspond with her, to discuss points of art history and practice his Italian, she agreed graciously. A few years later she was not surprised when he asked her to marry him. This was not the first offer she had ever received.

David went on to cause more emotional misery. One of his victims in the 1950s was Jeremy Thorpe, the future Liberal leader. Like Ben, Thorpe fell obsessively in love, and like Ben, was rejected as soon as the tearful scenes became – to David – boring and repetitive. Thorpe's biographer writes of a night in 1960 when Jeremy called on David, pleading to be let in as he stood under the windows of his lover's home. But the pleas and threats of suicide were unable to pierce a frozen heart and the door remained resolutely closed.[5]

* * *

A cartoon by Michael Rutherston that hung in Ben's bathroom. The caption reads: 'A few young bloods cling tenaciously to Oxford becoming younger and bloodier.'

A postscript to this story. The publisher asks me to look for images of myself with my father. I search and search as if by some spell the perfect photograph that was never taken will miraculously manifest itself. Or perhaps, again in a moment of magical thinking, I imagine that my favourite one of Ben and me together will reappear, the one I kept in my purse for years after he had died, the one that was stolen from my bag in a crowded Underground train. It doesn't of course, but in an old envelope I find something else, as if by compensation. The lost photograph of my father's lover feeding the pigeons in St Mark's Square.

I peer at it closely and notice how memory has played its tricks. David is not wearing brogues as I remembered, but open-toed sandals. Yes, his trousers are baggy but his jacket is not casual, it forms the smart part of his two-piece suit. And then I had described the birds eating 'out of his hands' but it is only one hand that feeds them.

I place the photograph back in the old envelope. After showing it to some friends I put it to one side, to take up to the publishers. Two days later I look on my desk and it has disappeared again. I must have put it somewhere for safekeeping. Where could it be? I look everywhere I can think of. And then I console myself by remembering how my now elderly mother once saw the photograph a few years back and remarked, 'oh look at Derek,' (an admirer of hers in the 1950s), 'how handsome he was when he was young.'

Derek, David, who knows. But I am certain I found it among my father's papers, all those years ago.

Julie

'Do you think of yourself as more English or Italian?'

I am thinking about the question Ben asked when I was a teenager and we were playing the Truth Game on that train journey through France.

As a young child I would have answered 'Equally', although as I approached my teenage years I leant towards my English side, for it was 'cool' to be associated with London. I had a Backing Britain poster on my bedroom wall in Florence and sneered at bad Italian pop music.

Now when I tell of growing up in Italy people tend to envisage days of endless sun and heat, of congenial meals taken with the extended family under shady, vine-roofed pergolas. 'But it wasn't like that,' I want to say, bristling at the stereotypical image of 'typical' Italian life.

By the time I arrived in Florence in 1962 aged six, my parents were communicating via telegrams and divorce lawyers. My Italian mother had taken me away from my English father and his country, but that, she told me later on, was what he had wanted. He was no longer a 'gentleman' in her eyes, for he was selfish and had acted ignominiously. He was unable to cope with family life, she said, because it was incompatible with a 'bachelor' lifestyle. I missed him but although he never came to visit me, I did not feel forgotten. Letters, cards and presents would arrive, flashes of paternal love squeezed into envelopes and parcels marked by his spidery writing, with postage stamps I carefully cut out to stick into childish books marked 'Francobolli'.

Occasionally I felt 'different' and sad for not having a daddy around or siblings to play with, but I was not particularly lonely. I had friends. Most were at school, but some, like Julie Schechtman, were made at home. I was seven when I met Julie, and she was slightly older. We lived at the same address for a year in the 1960s, until she returned with her parents to the US. The Schechtman family occupied the top floor of Via Romana 34, just south of Piazza Pitti. My home was in a separate apartment on the ground floor shared with my Italian mother and grandparents, Nonno and Nonna. Between Julie and me was the restaurant of the Pensione Annalena where we all took our meals.

It was in that dining room that I first saw this American Alice in Wonderland, and I desperately wanted her to be my friend. She was petite and delicate-looking, with a brightly intelligent face and long fair hair held back by a wide hairband. I, on the other hand, was tall for my age, with dark hair in braids, but I too wore a hairband. We seemed to have something else in common. I was an only child, and I swiftly observed that she did not appear to have any siblings either. I noticed these things. It is only recently that I found out that a sister, ten years older than Julie, had stayed behind in the US to go to university. I learnt this with a strange twinge of disappointment, as if I had been misled in some way. That somehow the bond was diminished.

Over fifty years later, reminiscences are shared as Julie and I rekindle our friendship through social media, then email. It is as if we have never lost touch despite years of separation and little contact in the intervening decades, apart from the odd letter.

What was her experience of being a little foreign girl in Florence, I ask her? What did that feel like? Why was her family there for a whole year? In our bubble of childish friendship none of this mattered. But now I want to mine her memories, to see the parallels and differences between her story and my own, to find out what she thought of my eccentric, multi-generational family with no daddy, and to remember how I viewed hers.

Why do I feel the need to discover these histories now, so many years later? Where does it come from, this preoccupation with the past and the people I used to know? Perhaps I feel they hold clues to why I have become the person I am and why certain things have happened in my life. But it's more than that. I'm curious to unearth the stories of those I remember, the stories I did not see.

Central to my story with Julie is Irma. I want my childhood friend to tell me about her, to fill me in, as I believe she may know more.

Irma was the waitress who worked in the hotel dining room. She was my first crush, before the little boys at school became more interesting. Crush in the widest sense of the word: she was the object of my unconditional love, and was someone I thought about and needed and became attached to without really knowing anything about. She was a steadfast, regular presence in my life for the four years I lived with my grandparents and I saw her more regularly than my own mother who was so often away on research trips, working. It was Irma who always looked pleased to see me, it was she who would comment on a new dress or toy or cheer me out of a bad or tearful mood. She offered consistency in an unstable world.

Irma was probably in her forties then, my mother's age, although hard work may have made her appear older. I remember thinning black hair with traces of grey and the beginning of lines on her face. My mother characterised her as a 'plain woman', a description that now makes me cringe with its dismissive disregard. But for Luisa aesthetic beauty was of paramount importance whether in works of art or in human beings. To be unaesthetically pleasing was as offensive to her as a bad taste or smell. She would readily admit this, 'I am an art historian after all, I need to see beauty around me.' If, as an adult, I wore clothes she didn't think went together, it would seriously disturb her. 'Your outfit fits you like *un cavolo a merenda*,' she would say, quoting an Italian expression meaning 'a cabbage for tea'.

Irma was not beautiful but the warmth of her personality made her so to me. And she certainly wasn't vain. I never saw her with make-up applied or dressed in anything but the uniform of her occupation: black dress, little white apron and flat black shoes. I can visualise her so clearly, coming towards me, her tone welcoming and affectionate to me, respectful to my mother and grandparents. I wish I could remember the exact sound of her voice – Florentine inflected, presumably, while Julie's must have been east coast American. But recollecting sound is, for me, so much harder to grasp than the visual images imprinted in my memory.

She was sweet to Julie too, with her affectionate nicknames, *Topo* (Mouse) and *Tesoro* (Treasure). And so when emailing my friend I ask questions about Irma. As a child had Julie been aware of Irma's background, maybe through hearing her parents talk about her? Although as my own family showed no interest in her, why should Julie's? Nonno would have said 'she is a waitress, here to serve us meals and that is all, why do you care?' But I really want to know what her life was like and how it continued after we had left.

Julie's memories are sketchy but she is sure that Irma had an adult son and that she lived with Giuliano, the other waiter who worked at the Pensione. Could Giuliano have been her husband? Her lover? Julie and I agree that seems unlikely. Giuliano appeared so much younger and rather lazy. He was a *buono-a-niente* (good-for-nothing) in Nonno's words. Surely the wonderful Irma would not have chosen him as a partner? Perhaps Giuliano was a younger brother. Perhaps it was purely a financial arrangement between colleagues and the accommodation they shared came with the job.

In fact I'm not sure Julie is that interested in Irma, but for me the unanswered questions remain. What could have happened to the father of Irma's son? He was never in evidence. Perhaps he had died in the war. Perhaps Irma had been abandoned by her lover after discovering she was pregnant. Perhaps they had married but then separated – not divorced because there was no divorce in Italy at the time. Perhaps they were prevented from living together. Perhaps he visited her during her time off, away from the prying eyes of little girls like me.

Perhaps, perhaps.

Not finding answers makes me want to create a story for her, to tie up the loose ends. It is as if my imagination wants to fill in the blanks when there is nothing else to go on. The painter Delacroix once wrote in his journals (in 1859), 'Even when we look at nature, our imagination contributes to the picture,' and I want to replace brushstrokes with words, inventing, linking, imagining, when facts are not available.

I would like to provide her with a happy ending. To find her living contentedly somewhere in ripe old age surrounded by loving grandchildren. But she is – or was, for it is likely she is dead by now – a real person, not a fictional character. I pray she was treated well and did not feel trapped by her situation. I trust she had somewhere comfortable to rest after her long working hours and later on, when she became too old to run around the dining room of the Pensione. I hope people were kind to her, as she was to me all those years ago.

The first thing Julie recalls is the cold. She knows Florence isn't always a warm and balmy place. It can be bitter in November, especially in houses designed for intense heat. Marble floors and wooden shutters are not conducive to cosiness. The high-ceilinged rooms Julie and her parents lived in were spacious but had no central heating. Julie remembers a little coal stove in a corner that struggled to keep the place warm so her parents bought an electric heater to get dressed in front of. One day Julie leaned in too closely and – zip! Her waist-length hair was singed up to her shoulders.

'All was made of stone that radiated a humid cold back out,' Julie writes, and I know exactly what she means, even if I associate the word 'humid' with steamy, oppressive heat. A kind of airless damp permeated the whole building. Stone was everywhere: worn smooth up the grey stairs, patterned with black and white on the apartment floors. And then that familiar smell, the smell of stone and plaster that years later became like a fragrance in Julie's memory.

Julie came from a musical family. Her mother was a singer but had also won a Fulbright prize to pursue her PhD in musicology. This was another thing Julie and I had in common – a busy, academic, working mother, a rare thing in 1963. The subject of Mrs Schechtman's doctoral dissertation was Francesca Caccini, a Florentine singer, composer, poet and music teacher from the early Baroque era; the daughter of one of the founders of a new form of music – opera. In fact Julie's mother was as multi-talented as her subject, sharing the same accomplishments: poet, singer, music teacher. And beautiful too, fair and slim, with a natural poise and elegance.

Like mine, Julie's father Saul was often absent, but unlike Ben, not permanently so. He was a conductor and composer and had been appointed musical director for the first French production of an American musical in Paris called – in translation – *Comment réussir dans les affaires sans vraiment se fatiguer*. 'How to Succeed in Business Without Really Trying' was a satirical look at American office life and had been a smash hit on Broadway. When every few weeks Saul Schechtman would return to Florence from Paris to see his family, he would go through the script and the songs for Julie's entertainment.

Saul was adventurous and charismatic. In 1960 he had been musical director on a production of *My Fair Lady* that comprised the first cultural exchange between the USSR and the US. It was extraordinary to have been to Russia at that time. He had also conducted in Scandinavia and Iceland. He would tell stories, like the time he was seated next to Ingrid Bergman at a dinner party. She had been badly treated by the American press over her affair with Roberto Rossellini and regarded Americans with suspicion, but Saul was proud to have thawed her coldness by coaxing, 'Come on, where's that famous smile?' She couldn't resist his charm, and smiled.

All this I would not have understood aged seven. But I knew he was a nice man. Looking back at a photograph of him now I see a big, balding extrovert with a broad, mobile face – not conventionally good looking but expressive. Back then I simply knew he made you feel happy and comfortable. I had a tendency to check out the fathers of my friends. Some were distant, some scary, some mischievously handsome and fun. I only saw my own father about once a year, but would compare. Ben was different somehow: older, awkward, less charming and interested in women, less competitive with men, not clued in to childish interests. He could take an age to say something. That did not matter. I carried private memories of him I didn't have to share.

The Schechtman family had been in Perugia learning Italian for a few weeks before arriving at the Pensione on 1 November, the feast day of *Tutti i Santi*. It was wet and gloomy and everything still felt unfamiliar to Julie as they drove into Florence. The buildings and pavements of the famous city were grey in the rain and Julie felt pangs of homesickness for her hometown in New Jersey. It wasn't just about the weather, after all her part of the US could be even colder. She disliked the food: olive oil made her feel ill and everything came with a coating of the stuff. Her parents searched for a store open on a national holiday where they might buy peanut butter, finally finding it in one that catered for foreigners. It was all Julie could consume at first. That and eggs. Endless hard-boiled eggs.

As an adult Julie would pine for the chance to live in Italy again, to be able to inhale the smells and hear the noises – even the bad ones. But during her first few months she was homesick. Her parents put her in English-language private schools where she was miserable so she was transferred to the neighbourhood elementary school. She was the only non-Italian there, and the only non-Catholic. She cried on the first day because the children sitting at their desks stared at her. Staring was a problem I had encountered too, and been unsettled by. It was an Italian thing, that's what people did. Men stared at young women and women looked at women too and children stared at anyone that looked slightly different from themselves. And they didn't look away when you stared back, as strangers did in London where to be openly curious was considered rude.

When Julie continued crying a teacher addressed a girl close by. Whereupon the girl stood up, came over, and gently kissed Julie's cheek. From then on she began to learn Italian and made friends – Daniela, Simonetta, Rossella, Francalia. Whereas for me Italian was the language I spoke at home. I had been sent to a private Italian school and hated it, and was much happier at the international school. All my friends were British and American. Paige, Karen, Carey, Holiss, Wendilee. These really were their names.

'I don't remember when you and I met,' Julie writes to me in one of her emails from the US. 'It must have been soon [after we arrived]. My family took our meals in the Pensione a couple of floors below, with the other guests. You sat with your grandparents and possibly your mother in a far corner of the dining room.'

I remember.

I remember walking up those stone stairs to the dining room every mealtime, being welcomed by Irma and guided with my family to our regular table in the corner of the room where I was able to observe. And one day noticing Alice in Wonderland with her parents sitting at another table and wondering whether I might go and say hello.

My mother and grandparents generally looked pained when I wanted to get up and make friends with the offspring of Pensione guests. Nonno was wary of strangers impinging on his life, especially if they were young children. Children meant noise and *confusione.* They came attached to parents who required acknowledgement. But I longed for distractions to ease the tedium between courses and seeing a girl my age and on her own made me restless and impatient to introduce myself.

'*Quella bambina é inglese*?' I asked Irma when she had served the family their soup and had come over to serve ours.

'*No, é Americana come Rick.*'

Rick was the nine-year-old who had provided amusement for a few weeks but had now gone back to California, leaving me with my first love letter, written on pink paper. 'Dear Vanessa, There is something I want to tell you, keep this a secret! (I love you!!) I made up a poem for you: I love you will you be mine?' Next to which I wrote in pencil, 'No'. I still have the note.

I smiled at the little girl with the hairband and she smiled back. She looked so pretty and approachable, and I sat there longing for her to be my friend.

'*Posso parlare con quella bambina*?' I pleaded, but it was only a few days later that Nonno – ever the patriarch – gave me permission to cross the dining room to her table. I was probably wearing my usual light-blue cardigan and blouse – my mother's preferred outfit for me – and Julie? I don't remember. But shyly I said hello, and Julie's parents smiled encouragingly. I hadn't known that in fact her parents had been urging her to speak to me but that she had been too shy. But once Nonno had given me the go-ahead we would wave to each other and if Nonno allowed it, we would chat before and after our meals.

Nonno referred to the Schechtman family as *gli Americani*. To be an American person or object carried a certain negative connotation for many Italians, however cultured and polite an individual, or useful and practical the object proved to be. For Nonno, the US meant a world of newness and brashness and vulgarity that he distrusted and wanted to be protected from.

'Towards me I sensed a faint disapproval radiating from your family but this may have been their habitual response to strangers,' Julie tells me. It is the oddest thing to learn of Julie's impressions of *us*, to imagine my family unit being observed and to have evidence of those observations. It is as if we have been playing our own Truth Game and I have asked her, 'what did you make of us?' And Julie is absolutely right, I recognise that suspicious approach she refers to – it was the response given to *all* my potential friends by my Italian family unless they were chosen by themselves; the narrowing eyes and shaking head, guilty before proved innocent, a bad influence, the wanting to keep everyone at arm's length.

But in the end they relented.

Monday 18 November 1963

> On Saturday Julie spent the afternoon with me. We played with my bubble blowing elephant. Today we had no school but went in the Duomo to pray for President Kennedy of America who was a good man and was killed.

I – unlike Nonno – loved everything and anything American. I loved singing the American national anthem at school. I loved Barbie dolls and Disney films, Halloween and peanut butter. My mother had been on a research trip to California and had brought me back a book about Disneyland. I scrutinised the photographs over and over again until the spine of the book collapsed and the pages began falling out. The longing to go to that place became a tangible ache. I felt it in my gut, all the more acute in the knowledge that I would never be taken there. The rides, the Disney characters, the fairy castle, it all seemed so glossy and shiny and desirable and impossibly unreachable.

Julie on the other hand had stopped being homesick and had settled in to Italian life. She insisted on being called Giulia instead of Julie. We listened to my records on the old gramophone in Nonno's library such as the traditional Neapolitan songs I loved, singing '*Saaaanta Lucia, Saaaanta Lucia*' or '*Funiculí Funiculá*'. We loved singing. Or we pirouetted and swayed our arms around the sitting room to the music of *Swan Lake* pretending to be ballet dancers. In a year or so my tastes would become less traditional, with The Beatles' 'All My Loving' replacing the Italian folk songs, but Julie had gone by then.

Christmas came and went, then Epiphany. My stocking from the old Befana – the old witch who traditionally brings presents to Italian children on 6 January – bulged with sweet coal. I had to explain to Julie that the custom of giving coal, albeit a candy version, to children instead of sweets was an indication of blame for bad behaviour. My manners were considered wanting, and this was my punishment. Julie was gentle and consoling, they weren't at all bad. In fact she thought they were 'exquisite' she said, using a very grown-up word. Even now, so many years later, she writes reassuringly about this event. 'You were much better behaved than I, so polite that I was absolutely staggered. If YOUR manners were considered reprehensible, what on earth must mine be like?'

By summer we were such firm friends that we felt miserable when kept apart during the week I was sent to a children's camp by the seaside. I didn't want to leave Florence and I didn't want to leave Julie and I certainly didn't want to go to La Corallina, the camp I was sent to every summer 'to escape the heat' (my mother's words) where I was not a name but a number, in my case number 116, still embroidered on to a small beach towel that lies folded in my bathroom cupboard to this day.

I recall that moment of separation more clearly than when Julie left to return to the US forever, a few months later. But then there was the terrible missing of her when it sunk in that she had gone for good. I was dejected without my friend upstairs. Irma tried to cheer me up. 'I am sure she will come back soon,' she said.

Julie and I wrote to each other on and off during the next few years. I kept all her letters. She told me about the first snows coming, about her dog Vicky, about her joining the Girl Scouts, about the singing lessons she was having. She asked after my family, she asked after Irma.

'I miss you and everyone at the Pensione! Tell Irma I did not have a chance to write to her.'

I remained living in that apartment with my mother and grandparents for another couple of years. I made friends with another little girl called Rebecca Williams who regularly holidayed with her parents at the Pensione – she *was* an only child and British rather than American, fair-haired too. I even stayed with her in Broadstairs a few times. But I never forgot Julie.

Then three bad things happened, one after another. Nonna died, Nonno became crazy and my mother depressed, all in the space of a few weeks. We had to leave the apartment on the ground floor and I can't remember ever saying goodbye to Irma. Possibly my mother wished to downplay our departure, possibly I downplayed it myself hoping that our leaving wasn't such a final thing.

I would be back. I would see both Julie and Irma again.

I did in fact, but not until eight years had passed. Julie wrote from the US that she was coming to Florence. She would love to see me. We arranged a rendezvous at the Pensione.

How strange that was. Eight years seem like nothing now, but how different a seven-year-old girl is from a fifteen-year-old one. I had evolved from sweet, accommodating child to troubled, sulky teenager. I was directionless, unhappy and self-destructive. I smoked, drank, did the minimum of schoolwork. All that really interested me were unreliable boys.

Julie was the reverse. She was positive and enthusiastic, a hard worker, involved in all the right extra-curricular activities at school. Even Julie's appearance was the opposite of mine. Light versus dark, clean versus grubby, new versus old. But these differences were forgotten as we met up in the street outside Pensione Annalena. Julie was staying there and she told me that Irma was still working as the hotel waitress.

As we climbed up those stone stairs I felt nervous with anticipation. Nothing had changed. The contrast of the coolness of stone after the summer heat outside was so familiar. The lingering smells of antique wood and polish as we entered the Pensione were the same. It was a time of day when the dining room was deserted but still there was Irma, welcoming, embracing us in turn, holding us away from her to say, 'let me have a good look at you.' She was shorter than I had remembered and older of course, with more strands of grey in her hair. And hunched – had she had a hunch before? But the warmth in her eyes was still there. I can't bring to mind what we spoke about or how long we stood there, only that she seemed moved by seeing us grown into young women. I do recall saying goodbye to her and walking back down those stone stairs with Julie and longing to ring the bell of what had been Nonno and Nonna's apartment. And feeling strangely excluded by the unfamiliar name on the brass plaque to the side of the door.

When, aged ten, I left the Pensione, possibly at the same time as my ranting, furious grandfather was placed in a nursing home – I was taken by my mother to stay with two elderly sisters called Nicky and Alda. Luisa had met them before her marriage when she was research assistant to the art historian Bernard Berenson. The older sister Alda had been Berenson's librarian and Nicky his companion.

I was sad to see my mother subdued and melancholic and tried to think of ways of cheering her up. I found that there was an American folk song, 'Little Boxes', that she liked me to sing. I don't know if I had learnt it from Julie or from my school, but its repetitive lines about little boxes on a hillside, little boxes made of 'ticky-tacky', would always cheer her up. Its digs at suburbanisation – little boxes all the same, a green one and a pink one and yellow one – were lost on me but I loved the nursery-rhyme quality of its slow rhythmic build-up and its jaunty tune. And what was tick-tacky? Only years later would I understand the genius of the song was in its disguise, in its appearance of childlike innocence.

Luisa would lie on the bed in the room we shared and say, 'sing me the song Vanessa,' and I would sing, and when I came to the end of the song I would start from the beginning again. One evening when we had retired to the sitting room after dinner, my mother told our hosts about the song she loved to hear me sing. They encouraged me to perform it, but I didn't want to, I was shy and anyway it was our special song, only for my mother's ears. But they kept pressing me: 'Sing the song, come on, sing the song.' I could see their expectant expressions willing me to get on with it, becoming impatient with the wait. There was no way out. I took a deep breath and opened my mouth. But I couldn't sing. A tiny squeak broke in the middle of the first line, '*Little box...es*'.

Nothing else came out. I had simply dried up.

Alda's old face cracked into laughter. 'Well, that's not much of a song is it? What a lot of fuss about nothing.'

My face was burning. I turned, tears flowing, and ran down the corridor and into our bedroom, where I threw myself on to my bed. My mother followed, finding me with my face in the pillow crying out over and over, 'I shall never EVER sing that song. I shall never sing any song, ever.'

I tell Julie of this childhood experience after reading the account she has sent me of her career. Julie became an opera singer, singing and recording in northern Europe. This was not surprising, considering her family background. I too followed the interests and profession of my art historian parents, having initially rejected anything to do with art and art history.

She tells how, as a young woman, she went to Germany to audition to various opera houses before she became established as a soprano. 'The auditions were mostly painless,' she writes. 'But I'll tell you: one of the first times I sang for someone in a semi-public setting, it was in a home economics class. I picked "Edelweiss", not realising it would never be the sort of song I would easily sing in public. Opera was psychologically easier. And it was to a bunch of sneering teenage girls who laughed when I broke on a note and I ran out of the room. It took me ages to live that disgrace down.'

Julie gives me the names of some of her recordings. I order a compilation of arias, the cover of which features her dressed in a wig and eighteenth-century costume. As the CD begins, the agility of her voice fills every corner of the room and I close my eyes, feeling the music, remembering the two of us over fifty years ago in dressing-up clothes, dancing around Nonno's library, hoping he would let us be, until the record came to its natural end.

I never saw Irma again or learnt what happened to her after the 1970s. I am wondering now whether I have attributed more space and significance to her in my childhood than she actually occupied.

Why would I not have contacted her again after I met her as a teenager, if she had meant so much to me? It seems only with hindsight that I want to allow myself the luxury of imagining that we had a bond, that I was as important to her as she was to me. That would indeed be comforting. And so I shall convince myself it is the truth.

Mr Right

At first I named him Sebastian because his real name was unknown to me. I felt it suited him. The images of Saint Sebastian in the Renaissance paintings I was studying combined virility and frailty into an ideal of male beauty attractive to a girl of twenty-one. A handsome youth wearing only a diminutive loincloth, his hands tied to a tree, his body pierced by arrows, with no pain distorting his beautiful features: there was something appealing about a brave but vulnerable martyr, waiting to be rescued.

I had first noticed my living Sebastian, not naked and tied against a tree, in the smoky environment of a university Common Room. It was easy to observe him as he sat slightly apart from the other students, self-contained and engrossed in his book, removed from the chatter that filled the room. He was lanky, fair-haired and boyishly pretty, dressed in a plain jumper and baggy trousers, with a scarf loosely thrown around his neck. He sat as if unaware of his beauty, and I was smitten.

From then on I regularly scanned the Common Room to check out his proximity as I queued to get my coffee between tutorials. If he was there he tended to be alone but close, languidly slumped in one of the old armchairs to the left of the cafe area, absorbed by his reading and seemingly indifferent to the bustle of his surroundings. His neck was always covered by the same scarf that I longed to steal and wrap around my own, to know his smell, to breathe him in.

For some time I had no context in which to place him – no friends, no gestures, no voice. To me he was just a flawless face and body in repose: a living work of art. Gradually I began to attribute all manner of romantic traits to his personality. He must surely be sensitive, poetic, imaginative, thoughtful, introspective, because to all appearances that is what he indicated, detached as he was from any social engagement or interaction. In my imagination the book in his hands was a nineteenth-century French novel, maybe something by Stendhal or Balzac, the heroes described in its pages a poor reflection of this living object of desire.

It was my fourth and final year at university. The previous academic year I had spent in Venice as part of my university course, but my time in that city had come to an abrupt end when my father had died, suddenly and shockingly. He had literally 'dropped dead' from a pulmonary embolism in Leicester Square Underground station after an evening out with friends. I was struggling. My relationship with my mother had deteriorated and a troubled, 'on-off' affair had ended after years of unhappiness and recriminations on both sides.

I wasn't looking for another boyfriend; I didn't want one. I had found all the security and contentment I needed living with my friend Ed in an early-Victorian terrace, high above Brighton.

It was Ed who had secured the accommodation, a basement flat attached to one of the elegant whitewashed houses that overlooked the town. The owner was a professor of American Studies, father of Ed's friend Shay, who lived with his much younger second wife in the spacious quarters upstairs. Ed and I had come to an agreement – I could share with him in return for making my father's flat available when he wanted to stay in London.

Our Brighton home was dark but comfortable. I occupied a room at the front, which required me to walk through Ed's bedroom to get to the kitchen and bathroom at the back, but this didn't bother us because we were so completely relaxed with one another. When my mother quizzed me over my living arrangements I explained that I was sharing with a friend called Edward. She appeared concerned.

'But what do you do...' she hesitated.

'What do you mean what do I do?'

Luisa looked uncomfortable. 'What do you do,' she asked in her strong Italian accent, 'You know... about not having the babies?'

'The babies?' I repeated blankly, and then her train of thought dawned on me.

'Oh no! No, no, he's homosexual,' I explained chirpily, as my mother still only used the term 'gay' in the old-fashioned sense.

She frowned when I said this, as if it might be a disappointment. She could not have been more wrong.

Ed was the perfect housemate. He loved cooking and I loved food. We shared a passion for chocolate brownies and would regularly set off after supper to Browns in the Brighton Lanes, where the brownies were served with a dollop of whipped cream on the side. We would gulp them down hastily, as if someone might catch us, while joking about our guilty secret. As well as a love for brownies we shared a sense of humour and a slight hypochondria. We cared for one another when ill and told each other our troubles, and we remain the closest of friends to this day, even though now separated by an ocean.

Back then Ed's drawl, stylish clothes, frizz of black hair and soulful, mischievous eyes made him the coolest person I knew. His American father worked for military intelligence, his mother was from the Philippines. Ed had been born in Austria, grew up in Munich but had been living in Paris. I liked the fact that his outlook was international rather than parochial, his background classless. He was four years older than me and had 'lived' life a bit.

He understood things.

So naturally I revealed all to him about my obsession with Sebastian, and in the telling and retelling the infatuation took a tighter hold. One day I pointed him out and Ed whispered, 'hmmm, he looks nice...' accompanied by a slightly raised eyebrow and grin.

It was meant as a friendly response yet I panicked a little as the thought came to me, 'what if Sebastian is gay?'

He certainly had an androgynous look about him.

Reassurance came when I saw him walking around campus in the company of a red-haired girl – clearly a girlfriend. Dismayed but resigned, as the girl was in every sense the opposite of me. She was voluptuous and exuberant, dressed in brightly-coloured clothes, with a loud, infectious laugh. She was a presence. I was tall, thin and dark, and shyly self-conscious to the extreme – an absence. I decided it was fanciful to think there was any possibility in meeting him, let alone having a relationship.

It was late May and I was revising for a difficult history exam when Ed came bursting into my bedroom.

'I've found out who he is!'

'Who who is?' I asked, looking up from my books.

'Sebastian of course, who else? And you won't believe what he's studying!' Ed laughed, savouring the moment.

I let my pencil drop on to my notebook.

'Oh God, who is he? How the hell did you meet him?'

'I have my ways!'

Ed then announced that he had got us invited to supper that evening by a mutual friend.

'I don't know if that's a good idea…um…' I stammered, 'I've got an exam tomorrow morning, I really should carry on revising.'

'Come on, don't be boring,' coaxed Ed who – unlike me – was sociable and always happy to meet new people. 'You're coming. I've set it all up now.'

And then he revealed Sebastian's name, the first part concealed here to retain a small measure of anonymity. But his surname amused us.

'Wright!' repeated Ed. 'See – he's "Mr Right". It's meant to be!'

The name stuck.

'So what is Mr Right studying? And what about the girl with the red hair?'

'You won't believe it. They are both doing art history, like us but in the year below. The girl is called Judith.'

'How suitably biblical!'

'But apparently they're no longer girlfriend and boyfriend. I've discovered everything.'

I was nervous at the supper, especially as Ed had contrived to get me seated next to Mr Right. I couldn't think of anything to say. I could hardly eat, which was very unlike me. Everything I tried to swallow seemed to get stuck halfway down my throat, as did my words when I attempted to speak.

Mr Right was softly spoken and distracted and it was only towards the end of the evening that he even acknowledged me. He was showing the assembled group a trick that involved circling one's fingers around the palm – or was it the wrist – of the other hand. I can't remember what this was supposed to demonstrate. Was it about sensation or gesture or simply a party trick? Was he making a point about communication or deception? I have no idea. My eyes glazed over and it was only when Ed nudged me with his foot under the table that I took another gulp of wine to fortify myself and held my wrist up in his direction.

'How do you mean?' I asked as he turned and took my hand in his. He looked into my eyes as he ran his finger around the surface of my hand and said something insignificant. I was mesmerised, without having any sense of what he was talking about. But the attraction was clearly not reciprocated, and this was problematic. There was nothing I could see in his eyes but an eagerness to make a point.

That night I couldn't sleep. Round my head swirled the few innocuous phrases that had passed between us. The fact that for a moment or two I had entered into his consciousness, that I had existed for him, was enough. Oh, and the sweetness of remembering the electricity engendered by his finger circling on my skin, the misery of knowing that no further meeting had been arranged. Then the frustration of wanting more than anything in the world to be funny and clever and irresistible, or at least for some sort of magic to happen so that the mundanities that had come out of my mouth that evening would lure him into feeling something towards me. If only I had that power.

The next morning I was sitting sleepily hung-over at a desk in the examination hall, staring at questions I couldn't answer. The historical facts I had been cramming into my head for weeks had all but disappeared. The exam paper might as well have been in Mandarin. I was hot, I was tired, my mind kept drifting; the connection between my brain and my pen was lost. I was unable to consign a single word to paper. All that kept coming into my head was Mr Right circling his finger around the palm of my hand.

Disaster. Concentrate. Focus. Mustn't mess up.

I asked the invigilator if I could go to the bathroom. He looked up from his papers and frowned as he nodded. 'Be quick,' he said.

Alone behind the closed door, I put my head in my hands. The voice was there, *you idiot, you've fucked up.* Earlier that day I'd had some notes tucked into the pocket of my jeans, but I'd taken the crumpled scrap of paper out for one last look outside the exam room and now it was in my bag, on the floor by that desk I had left behind in the hall. I smiled at the irony of this. It would have been so easy to cheat but I'd bungled even that opportunity.

I shall go back and pull myself together and everything will be fine.

I was in the hall again, looking at the clock. We were over half way through the exam time and all I had written down were a few sentences of gibberish. The sound of shuffling papers and the odd cough filled the room. The girl in front of me was hunched over her paper scribbling furiously. I hated her. Time passed.

Damn you Mr Right. Damn me. Damn everything.

I got up slowly, picked up my bag and told the invigilator that I was leaving.

'Are you sure? There is still half an hour to go.'

Yes I'm sure.

And then I walked slowly across the campus, each step away from that hall a reminder of my failure. I was trying to control the anxiety that was rising through me, trying to concentrate on putting one foot in front of the other, but it felt as if at any moment I might trip and fall flat on my face. I found myself stumbling into the health centre, going into a full-blown panic attack as I slumped into a chair in the waiting room. Dr Ryle, the university psychiatrist I had seen at various points of crisis during the last few years, was called. I was given a room with white walls and a bed and a desk and I spent the next few days there 'in isolation', first sleeping, then doing the exam papers that were delivered to the health centre. At regular intervals meals were brought to me on metal trays.

'Don't worry Vanessa,' Dr Ryle reassured me at the end of the week as I was being discharged. 'You have a great quality. Resilience. You will be all right.'

Now that contact had been made I was able to nod and say hello to Mr Right whenever I saw him around the university, often 'accidentally' bumping into him when reports came my way that he was in the library or refectory. But our exchanges never got much beyond the level of 'how you doing?' Once when we stopped to greet each other I asked him what he was reading and he brought the book he was carrying out from under his armpit. Expecting to see something intense and intellectual, or at least a title from the art history reading list, I was taken aback when he revealed it was a book on the social history of the British nanny. So much for French literature!

'He's just a shy public schoolboy,' I thought. How different he was from the angry working-class boys or politically active middle-class ones I was usually attracted to. Even the unfashionable period of painting he was most absorbed by – eighteenth-century British – made him appear separate, not of the same tribe, as if he was at the wrong university. My friends' interest in art and literature was rooted in the twentieth century.

There was something unworldly and guarded in his personality that made me desperate to show him that I could be trusted, if only he would let me in. I could tell he liked me but it was a polite, respectful, distant, non-committal kind of liking. I wanted more than that, I wanted to beguile him. But the more desperately I wanted this, the more plodding and unnatural I became in his presence. I tried to make him real, human – to bring him down from the pedestal I had put him on. But my infatuation had dehumanised him to such an extent that he had become the art object – the Sebastian, the Apollo – I had reduced him to being.

Things came to a head on a warm summer evening during that short interlude when exams are over but the academic year has not yet ended. With no deadlines to worry about, social arrangements became loose, and one balmy evening a group of us, including Ed and Mr Right, found ourselves hanging out on the beach after a session in the pub. Conversation was always slightly stilted between Mr Right and me, but we had been getting on reasonably well and suddenly – flushed by alcohol and frustration, with recklessness surging in my veins – I spontaneously grabbed his arm.

'Come on, let's go swimming!' I shouted as I ran fully clothed into the sea, dragging him behind me. He was game and followed me into the freezing grey water. We splashed around a bit before emerging back on to the beach, dripping and cold, to the cheers of the assembled group.

A plan was taking shape. We had ended up far from my flat but near Mr Right's house, in a different area of Brighton. I exaggerated my teeth chattering and Mr Right gallantly suggested we all go back to his house to warm up. Our group sat around drinking hot tea, Ed grinning as I appeared from another room wearing a large, old shirt that Mr Right had found for me to change into. Were there trousers too? That seems unlikely, though we were both thin, but the essential thing was that I was wearing Mr Right's shirt like a second skin, while mine hung to dry in a bathroom or kitchen somewhere.

I was emboldened by the frisson this gave me to ask, 'Do you mind if I stay a while, to make sure my clothes are dry?' It seemed that I would win whatever he answered, for either I would get to stay or I would be leaving wearing something of his that would need to be returned.

The book on nannies was lying on a table and I picked it up. We managed a conversation of sorts on the subject. People were drifting off home and then Ed said he was tired too and he must set off, not meeting my eye, suggesting to the remaining few that they might come with him.

Everyone was standing and collecting their things and then they were all gone and I was being offered another tea I didn't really want and talking more about nannies. Had he perhaps had a nanny as a child of whom he was very fond? Who knows, but I remember looking at his perfect face, watching him talk but not hearing him, and wondering how the evening – now night – would end.

It was late. He yawned. 'Shall I make you up a bed?' he said suddenly, perhaps despairing that I would never leave, but that interpretation did not strike me then. Five minutes later we were facing each other as we put a spare sheet on a mattress on the floor by his bed, and as the second sheet fanned up in the air, I thought it's now or never.

'Can I ask you something?'

'Of course.'

I took a deep breath.

'Would it be all right…' I made a cringing expression. 'What I mean is…' I had to come out with it. 'Um… can I sleep with you?'

He looked bemused as he answered quickly and rather sweetly, 'that would be lovely…' and we stood self-consciously, the corners of the spare sheet still in our hands, until we it let go and climbed into his bed.

There was nothing particularly memorable or passionate about our encounter but when later we sat up, propped up by pillows, we chatted amicably, discussing our summer plans. He was going to Spain, I was joining other friends in Greece, but he alluded to a potential future together, to us writing and keeping in touch over the summer, to meeting when he returned to Brighton for his final academic year. 'I'll come and see you in London and you can come back and visit me here,' he said.

I was euphoric.

He had put his arm around me. 'You know,' he said tenderly, 'this is all such a surprise. I never expected this to happen.'

And then I made *the mistake*. I told the truth.

I laughed and said, 'oh God, if only you knew,' and recounted how desperate I had been for this to happen, how I'd spotted him six months previously and developed a huge crush and how Ed had done what he could to bring us together, and about all the many times Ed and I had manoeuvred chance encounters with him, and my impulse decision led by desperation to drag him into the sea, and as the words tumbled out I felt his arm tense up and lift away from my shoulders. Dread seeped into my bones.

What have I done? How stupid can I be?

It was getting light. He got out of bed and made some coffee and reappeared with my clothes – 'I think they are dry,' he said in an off-hand way and I took them from his hand and felt like crying.

He walked me home along the seafront but we hardly spoke. Part of me had wished to bring my humiliation to an end and say goodbye there and then in his bedroom but I also wanted to hang on to the fantasy of being in a relationship with him for as long as possible. We arrived at my house, Ed grinning as if I had come home with a trophy won, but I was on edge and Mr Right quickly made his excuses – he was tired, he had to get back – and he was gone.

It didn't end there. We managed a relationship of sorts over the next six months – a friendship with sex attached, if you like. He had sent me a couple of postcards from Spain during the summer and I wrote back about my time in Greece. And when autumn and then winter came he visited me in London on a few occasions. I was sharing my father's flat with my friend Minky now. Ed had left Europe to live in New York.

We would visit museums and galleries, art being the binding interest we shared. But we would walk around exhibitions, separate and uncommunicative. If I went to Brighton to see him we would end up in cafes or restaurants, me regularly unable to eat or speak, longing to do both but tied in knots by nerves and the wish to make a good impression. I was so desperate for him to like me but everything I said was filtered through a critical dialogue in my head that rendered my conversation stiff and rigid, as if every word had been dipped in starch. My stuttered responses would return to haunt me during sleepless nights as I blushed in the dark, recalling my abject failure in captivating him with anything I might have to say. One vividly awful evening in a popular restaurant involved a jolly Italian waiter regularly interrupting our stilted exchanges by waving a giant pepper grinder above our heads and sighing 'ah, fresh young love…' The pepper fell like a dusting of black snow on my untouched spaghetti. I wondered whether to whisper in

Italian, *'lasci fare'*, let it be, to let him know how sadly inappropriate he was being.

I had become friends with Judith, his ex-girlfriend. I liked her and when one day she invited me round, I accepted and we sat in her student house, in a large room surrounded by red velvet drapes and cushions, drinking tea and after a while she said, 'come on, enough, let's talk honestly', because neither of us had mentioned our mutual entanglements with Mr Right. I admired her straight talking but was slightly in awe, as she had the upper hand. She was funny though, and we bonded, laughing over his idiosyncrasies. I think he knew this because he became nervous about me meeting her and perhaps revealing too much. When he stayed over with me a few times in London he pressed me not to tell her.

Not surprisingly he began breaking arrangements. Promises to come and see me were not followed up. One day, frustrated by not having heard from him for a while, I wrote him an angry letter asking him what was going on. He answered that he had got back together with Judith. I had suspected this, of course he had, he had previously enjoyed a proper relationship with her, she had meant so much to him for so long. What else could I have hoped for? I didn't blame him. He had never declared any commitment to me, never promised me anything. The only thing I could accuse him of was perhaps a lack of frankness, a trace of weakness. But I think he had only been trying to protect my feelings. I withdrew, feeling rejected, pining in the privacy of empty rooms, not so much for the relationship I'd lost but for the one I'd never had with him.

A couple of years later I saw him from the top deck of a London bus, walking purposefully along the street below. The bus was stuck in traffic and – heart beating fast – I knew I could just run down the stairs and jump off, pretending to bump into him. 'What a coincidence!' I would say, flicking back my hair. But I knew that would be playing the old game, and what would be the point? He might say, ever polite, 'how nice to see you, can I give you a call?' like the time he had done when I bumped into him outside a cinema, but intending it in that English 'let's do lunch' sense that really means 'let me get away from you as quickly as possible in a dignified way'.

For a long time I berated myself for my stupidity and bad judgment in making *the mistake*. What had I been thinking? Who knows what might have happened if I'd kept my mouth shut. Possibly – probably – nothing at all. But, just in case, I made sure in subsequent relationships never to disclose my true feelings unless evidence of love and irrefutable commitment from the partner had already been established. I had learnt a lesson: best to hold it back. Andrew, my husband, complains that I have hardly ever declared my love for him – my twisted logic convinces me that even after decades of marriage and two children this might frighten him off. You never know.

Fast-forward twenty-five years. It was an ordinary Monday morning and I was clearing up after the school run. I was in the bathroom sorting out the washing when Andrew appeared in the doorway.

'I've got a name for you,' he said as I looked up. And then he said the name in full. '**** Wright.'

I hadn't thought about Mr Right for years, but hearing the name froze me to the spot.

'You've gone white!' Andrew laughed and left the room.

I felt discombobulated the whole morning. At lunchtime Andrew explained. He had been chatting to a PR woman about a forthcoming interview – he was working as a business journalist at the time – and before they got on to discussing arrangements they engaged in polite conversation about how they had passed their respective weekends.

'We went to Brighton, where my husband spent his university years in the late 1970s,' she had said.

'Really? What a coincidence, my wife was at Sussex around then.'

'Well my husband studied the history of art...'

'How funny – my wife did too! I wonder if by any chance they knew each other?'

And then names were exchanged and when the telephone call was over Andrew had come upstairs to find me.

That evening I was running a bath when Andrew sought me out again.

'So what's the story with this Mr Wright?' he asked playfully.

I laughed, mock-melodramatically, rolling my eyes.

'Oh just someone who broke my heart.'

Except, to be honest, he didn't really, or at least he did only temporarily. And it was not his fault either. His only crime was not being the Mr Right I had invented, and longed for him to be. It was the construct not the real person I had fallen in love with.

As a wise friend said to me, many years later, 'He never stood a chance.'

Martyrdom of St Sebastian by Sandro Botticelli

2

FAITH

Malú

> I am not writing this for fun, but for several reasons which I will explain. (1) As I started by saying, because I want to tell the entire truth. (2) Because I know of no truthful record of such a connection – one that is written, I mean, with no desire to appeal to a vicious taste in any possible readers: and (3) Because I hold the conviction that as centuries go on, and the sexes become more nearly merged on account of their increasing resemblances, I hold the conviction that such connections will to a very large extent cease to be regarded as merely unnatural, and will be understood far better, at least in their intellectual if not in their physical aspect. I believe that then the psychology of people like myself will be a matter of interest, and I believe it will be recognised that many people of my type do exist than under the present-day system of hypocrisy is commonly admitted.[6]

I WAS IN ITALY IN 2009 ON ONE OF MY REGULAR TRIPS TO VISIT my mother Luisa when my Italian cousin Malú texted to arrange a meeting. She lives in Turin but was passing through Florence and wanted us to meet her partner Simone and their two small children. Malú had tried to do this before but Luisa would not invite them in.

She disapproved.

Over breakfast in her antiquated kitchen I tried to change her mind and agree to see them.

'It's not natural,' she said with finality, as she spread her toast with anchovy paste. 'It's not fair on the children.'

* * *

Years ago, Luisa would never stop talking about Malú. For a while it was all, 'Malú drove me to this or that exhibition', 'Her research is developing so well', 'Malú says… Malú was telling me,' and so on, to the point that I became resentful of this girl I'd never met; a younger, better version of everything my mother wished me to be, and everything I was unable to deliver.

My Nonno was brother to Malú's Nonno, so Luisa was first cousin to Malú's father. I never knew that side of the family when I was growing up because they had remained settled in northern Italy while we were in Tuscany. But when Malú was a student of art history and needed to pursue some research in Florence, her father arranged for a meeting with Luisa – both a Florentine and a well-connected art historian. They hit it off immediately and from then on met up on a regular basis.

When Luisa finally introduced us on a hot day during a summer holiday, I surprised myself by liking her. She was twelve years younger than me, so at that time she would have been in her twenties. We met for lunch in a restaurant outside Florence, so we were on neutral territory. I was with Andrew and our two small daughters. She came with her sister Caterina.

Malú was quietly friendly without being gushy, straightforward without being blunt, and generally nothing like the person I had imagined. What had I imagined? A kind of 'Christie's Girl', a pejorative term I used for the sort of assistants Luisa had taken on when she worked for the auction house – groomed, efficient, upper class and, to me, boringly straight-laced – but who actually appeared to enjoy life rather more than I did. Once, in the 1970s, when Luisa had insisted I go to her hairdresser, I had been given lacquered tresses with flicked up ends in the style of the actress Farrah Fawcett-Majors. The sort of bouncy blow-dry I loathed. When I got back to Luisa's apartment I threw a tantrum. 'You're trying to turn me into a Christie's Girl,' I shouted tearfully, before slamming out of the door.

Malú had plain, centrally parted, unstyled dark hair like mine, and in her T-shirt, jeans and no make-up looked natural and unthreatening. She was also rather different to her sister Caterina, a sexy actress well known in Italy, who amused us by flirting outrageously with my bemused and very English husband. When we all said goodbye it was Malú who was warmer, despite having hardly spoken over lunch. She seemed to mean it when she insisted we make contact if we ever came to Turin.

A few years later that is exactly what we did. We arranged to meet her in a cafe in the centre of town. By then she had graduated and – funnily enough – was working for Christie's in Italy. This made me smile.

Over coffee and pastries she spoke about her work, and about the 'girlfriend' she lived with. She seemed happy and settled. When she left I turned to Andrew. 'Do you think she's a lesbian?' Not that it mattered, but the Italian word '*amica*' is ambiguous. It translates as 'girlfriend' without the connotations. But she kept talking about living with '*my* girlfriend' rather than '*a* girlfriend' and the way Malú's eyes smiled every time she mentioned her made me wonder.

Of course she was in a relationship with another woman, as her immediate family had guessed. My mother was not particularly interested in Malú's choice of partner, but what she could not accept was the arrival of children, once the couple became part of a larger family unit. And when I sat in her kitchen in 2009, explaining that Malú, who she liked so much, and her girlfriend Simone and their little girl and baby boy were passing through Florence, and wanted to drop in and say hello, Luisa would not allow it. She was adamant. Her own experience of homosexuality – my father's love of other men and his rejection of her – had embittered her. My attempts to persuade her to change her mind came to nothing.

Later that morning Malú texted once more to confirm the arrangements to meet for lunch. She wondered whether she might simply ring Luisa's doorbell on the way to the restaurant, family in tow, but I knew that was a bad idea. When she did ring the bell I turned to Luisa and said one last time, 'are you sure you won't see them? They're outside the building,' but her pursed lips were enough to answer the question. I ran down the stairs, and we walked to the family-run trattoria around the corner. There we were joined by my friend Ed, who had been staying in Fiesole, outside Florence, on a brief holiday from his home in San Francisco.

Malú was withdrawn and understandably unnerved by Luisa's behaviour. I was mortified. We tried to cheer ourselves up by ordering a lot of good food and wine. Once the children were settled and our hunger abated, I asked Simone, who is from Luxembourg, whether they had encountered much prejudice in Italy over their family configuration.

'Attitudes are slowly changing,' she answered, 'but it can be really hard.'

Then the two of them recounted – a bit in Italian, a bit in English – how they had had to go abroad to get treatment from a clinic in Holland so that Malú could be made pregnant by artificial insemination.

'I wanted to have the experience of pregnancy, of giving birth, of being the biological mother. It has been a long journey... but it was worth it!' Malú looked affectionately at her two beautiful children.

And so in between dealing with children and eating plates of pasta, they told their story. Ed joined in with his own account of his partner's family in Korea, of incomprehension and homophobia, and the hour or so we were there passed quickly. As we stood outside the restaurant saying goodbye, Malú gave me a book for Luisa.

'I would have liked to give it to her myself, but…' She shrugged, and I could see she was saddened.

Years later I try to recall details of the conversations we had that day. When we had sat in that restaurant over lunch, it was Simone who had spoken more, because Ed was present and Simone's English is more fluent. But I wanted to hear it from Malú.

I email her, explaining that I want to write about the issues thrown up by her experiences. She writes back straight away. 'Let's meet next time you come to Italy.'

So in the autumn of 2015, I break the journey to Florence in Milan. Malú says she will take the train in from Turin. We meet at a hotel, a palatial Art Deco affair on the other side of the square from the station. I have booked a table in the library. We ask for sandwiches as Malú hasn't had time to get lunch and she teases me over being so 'English' when I pour milk into my tea. 'In England I always took it with milk too!' and I protest back, 'no, in Italy I usually have it with lemon,' because I wish to appear more Italian. And then we are laughing because as she begins recounting her story, the piano music piped into the room (how odd to play music in a library) gathers momentum, sounding like the soundtrack to a sentimental film. The waiter comes and goes, and each time he promises to turn the music down and forgets to do so. He keeps bustling in as if he is checking up on us. It's as if he wants to hear Malú's story too.

I start by asking her bluntly if she was always attracted to girls.

'Yes, from a really early age. But like many of my generation, I didn't want to accept it. I had some relationships with boys. I was attracted to both girls *and* boys.'

I remember Luisa attributing Malú's interest in her girlfriend to a *delusione*, a 'disappointment', with a man. I was so irritated by the presumption that only by having failed relationships with men would a woman be attracted to her own gender. But Malú appears to read my thoughts.

'To be honest, men let me down,' she says. 'I seemed to be incapable of making an intimate connection in relationships with men, although I've had strong friendships with them. They interest me.'

At university and studying for her thesis, she fell in love with a girl she met playing football. Although the relationship didn't work out, at the time it felt overwhelming and she realised that it would only be with a woman that she would find happiness. There was another woman she fell passionately in love with, to the point of obsession.

'For three years I thought of her day and night. But she rejected me; she stopped speaking to me. I really suffered from this.'

Then she met Simone.

Simone had come to Italy, via university in Belgium, to work for the European Training Foundation, an agency of the European Union based in Turin that helps improve vocational training systems in non-EU countries. She grew up in a small town in Luxembourg where her parents worked in education. Like Malú, her first relationship was with a man but she knew in her heart that she was attracted more to women. It took a while before she came out to her parents but she did so before embarking on her first relationship with a woman.

'It never usually happens like that, but she is so honest...' Malú says proudly. 'Her parents left her alone.' I wonder later did she mean by this that they left Simone unsupported or in peace to get on with her life? In any case the father died when Simone was twenty-four. She dropped out of university and began working, coming to Italy shortly after.

For Malú there was no 'confession' or announcement to her parents. Her father Agostino had guessed that his daughter was gay and asked her about it when she had been with Simone for about a year. She never discussed the subject with her mother, knowing her father would do so.

I never knew Agostino but when Malú begins talking about him we remark on the characteristics he shared with my mother, even though they were cousins, not siblings, and not particularly close. Both were cultured, clever, bookish. Both manifested moments of frightening, explosive rage like their fathers had done before them, and at other times could be liberal and reasonable.

Agostino was a medical man, a respected gynaecologist. When his older daughter Caterina got pregnant aged twenty-one without knowing the identity of the father, he and his wife brought up the child as their own so that Caterina could pursue her acting career. He could be sympathetic and understanding, but at the next moment might turn nasty, taunting Malú's mother with accusations that had no basis in reality. Even so, despite the times he was domineering and cruel towards his wife, they had a strong bond. She adored him and was devastated by his death five years ago.

Like Agostino, Luisa had a terrible temper. Her rage was legendary. Many colleagues, relatives and friends have been on the receiving end of one of her tirades, whether directed at them or someone else. Her temper can flare up in seconds over anything, from someone disagreeing with her to being made to wait for something. She hates waiting. Once, over twenty years ago, she was made to stand a bit too long outside my daughter Rosa's playgroup while preparations were being made for the annual nativity play. I was mortified when she began shouting that this was 'intolerable', one her favourite English words. The other mothers stared – or worse, pretended not to stare – as I tried to calm her down, muttering excuses as if I were personally responsible for the delay.

Luisa was drawn to people who had a professional interest in art and this inevitably involved artistic friends who led unconventional lifestyles. Yet at times she could be judgmental and moralistic. I don't think she saw anything contradictory about these extremes of intolerance and liberalism. Basically she had an ability to pretend things did not exist if they did not fit in with her view of how things should or ought to be. Her way of explaining the failure of her marriage was that my father was a loner and impossible to live with. She never spoke – at least not to me – about his homosexuality. Maybe she thought this was 'protecting' me, that I might be ashamed or unsettled by the knowledge. Until Malú had children, Luisa could pass Simone off as a good friend and housemate. But when Malú wanted her to acknowledge her kids and accept that Simone was part of her family unit, this for Luisa was impossible.

Malú is philosophical when I reiterate how sad I am that despite her deep affection for Malú – and I know that affection runs deep – my mother could not bring herself to welcome them that time she and her family came to Florence.

'Do you not think that it's precisely to do with her relationship with your father and her refusal to accept his sexuality?'

'Yes, probably,' I answer. 'A denial of Ben's homosexuality; a denial of yours.'

I tell my cousin about the exchange of letters my parents wrote to each other in the late 1950s when they left the marital home on their work-related research trips. 'Ben was constantly writing about his unhappiness, that he could not be a "normal" husband. He wrote these letters for four years before Luisa agreed to a divorce. She seemed to be saying back, "don't be ridiculous, pull yourself together, of course we can't divorce."'

I go on to vent my frustration with Luisa's intransigence. She has entrenched beliefs she refuses to discuss, let alone begin to change. And she has a tendency to drop people she feels have disappointed or confused her, or have failed to live up to her expectations.

'I understand that so well,' says Malú. 'I also have the ability to cut off, to sever all ties when I have been hurt. I had it as a child, this sense of "you are not responding in the way I want you to, therefore I shall eliminate you from my life". My father had this trait too.'

It is a relief to be having this conversation. We both know our criticisms are tempered by filial love. We will not judge each other harshly. We are not saying a loved parent is a monster, just hard to fathom sometimes.

Fortunately both Malú's mother and father were supportive when she decided to have children. 'They could see I was unhappy and at some point I spoke to my mother about it. She was a gentle, creative person – she painted, she sang, she acted – and she was sympathetic to me. I wasn't taking the decision lightly, it was strange for me to think about having a child by an anonymous donor.' Because of her father's professional work in gynaecology, pregnancy and birth were very present in the family, and maybe this made discussing her longing to have a child with her parents easier.

Before meeting Simone, Malú had considered having a child with a particularly close gay friend of hers: someone who would be interested in being involved with the parenting. But once she had met Simone, it felt strange to choose to have a child with him. Then they turned to a gay friend of Simone's, thinking this would balance things, but there was some hesitation on the part of the friend's boyfriend. He wasn't convinced by the idea. Also for Simone, the thought of Malú and *her* gay friend sharing the parentage and upbringing of a child felt equally excluding. So they decided on an anonymous donor.

At first Simone had been ambivalent about the whole issue of them having children at all. She didn't have strong feelings either way about being a parent. It was Malú who pushed for it and because Simone was in love with her, she came round to the idea and wholeheartedly supported her decision.

So, I ask, how did the pregnancy come about?

'I knew I really wanted a child, but it was hard for me to approach a clinic and to come to terms with having my children by an anonymous donor. It was a very stressful time. I had a lot of doubts. But I had this friend from Milan who had been to a small clinic in Holland that also had some public funding, and she had given birth to a beautiful baby girl. My friend had had such a positive experience from this small clinic, where the sperm donors were all local to Leiden. So in 2004 Simone and I went there for an assessment with a psychologist and after a year on the waiting list I was called up.'

Did she know anything about the donor?

'I had asked for someone who would resemble Simone although obviously we didn't know anything about him – there isn't a catalogue to choose from! I have since wondered whether the children of my friend who used the clinic and my own might have had the same sperm donor. When the baby is born one can ask for an identikit of the donor. We compared identikits and it looks like my friend's children and mine might well be half-siblings. We would have to have DNA tests to be sure though.'

I tell Malú how when I met Simone for the first time I had been struck by the likeness between her and the children, despite no biological connection. Maybe it was something to do with the donor coming from Leiden, and Simone – being from Luxembourg – having a northern European appearance. Yes, she answers, others have commented on the physical resemblance, it's uncanny.

The first attempt at becoming pregnant, when Malú went to the clinic alone, was unsuccessful. Simone accompanied her to Leiden the second time, and this second attempt worked. Malú's voice is tender as she recalls the changes happening in her body in those early months of pregnancy.

'Simone and I used to go jogging and I remember it was the first time I lagged behind, whereas I had always been the faster one. I was tired but so happy.'

She pauses before adding, 'I wanted her [the baby] so much.'

It was a difficult birth. Seventeen hours of labour and then a Caesarean. A week before the baby was due she learnt that they were closing the Christie's office and that she no longer had a job.

'Simone was amazing, particularly having not taken the decision to have a baby herself. She was a rock in supporting me. I was depressed from losing my job and exhausted by the birth. I had difficulties with breastfeeding. And she continued to support me – us – for a while, both emotionally and financially, because the academic jobs I managed to get (teaching, writing) did not bring in much money. She is amazing, because she got very stressed and isn't that strong, she is actually quite fragile.'

Lisa was born in 2006, and two years later Malú gave birth to a boy, Eric, also by Caesarean. When they decided to have a second child they considered Simone taking her turn to become a mother. But Simone was indecisive so they agreed that Malú would carry the second one too. She became pregnant immediately.

Eric comes from the same sperm donor. One of the reasons Malú and Simone chose the clinic in Leiden is because at that time Holland was the only country that allows children to trace their sperm donor fathers when they are sixteen. They wanted to be honest to the children about their origins from the very beginning. They have close friends in Leiden and visit regularly.

'When Lisa was not yet two I was already pointing out the clinic to her.' Malú laughs. 'She would not have understood, but this is something that can slowly become richer with detail. I like the idea of the kids feeling connected, locating themselves in a geographical place. It's up to them what they decide to do when they are older.'

Despite Simone's initial ambivalence they are a strong, close family unit. And yet Malú was not able to have the treatment she wanted in Italy. And, at the time of writing, civil partnerships are not allowed there either. Same-sex couples living in Italy have no shared rights to property or inheritance, although this is in discussion.

'I'm surprised,' I say, 'that Italy should remain so backward. It seems a violation of human rights. After all, it is not the only Catholic country in Europe. Even Ireland has passed the law allowing civil partnerships. Malta too.'[7]

Simone has no rights as a co-parent as she is not seen as a co-parent in law. She can't pick the kids up from school without Malú giving written permission. And if she needs to take the children to hospital, she can't make any medical decisions on their behalf.

Malú was one of the founders in 2005 of an organisation called Famiglia Arcobaleno (Rainbow Family) that has linked up with other gay rights associations to try and get outmoded regulations changed. There are 800 members, not counting the children. It's doubled in two years and is still growing.

At Lisa's first nursery school in Turin, everyone avoided mentioning that Lisa had two mummies. The teachers never included Simone, and Malú felt that in front of the other children they manifested a reserve, almost shame, about Lisa's 'mummies'. Then they moved house and Lisa went to a new nursery where the teachers were more open-minded. Malú organised a workshop that dealt with confronting homophobia. 'If you dig around, homophobia is there,' she says. 'But now I have become friends with other mums. The kids are much more integrated.'

I ask whether Lisa appears to feel any different from her school friends or misses having a family that is more traditionally configured.

'I couldn't really tell you if I'm honest,' Malú answers. 'Only a few days ago I felt something was wrong – in the way a mother can sense something being not quite right – and I asked her, "Do you mind not having a daddy?" and she answered, "Yes." I tried to explain that all families are different and it depends on the kind of parents one has, the main thing is that they are caring. That is what being a family is all about. She is the kind of kid who can sometimes be manipulative, like saying she has tummy ache to get out of going to school, making all sorts of excuses, so maybe it didn't mean anything. But I want her always to know that she can talk about what is worrying her, and not think that she has to hide her feelings. It's far better to confront issues as they come up, than pretend they aren't there.'

And how is Malú as a mother? Do she and Simone have different roles?

'I've noticed that in the last year it has really changed. We were like a traditional heterosexual couple – I looked after the house, had supper waiting for Simone when she got home, put the children to bed and all that. But for the last two and a half years that I have worked [at a different auction house] it's become much more balanced. To the point where she would quite like to have a break and cut down her working hours. I think she wants it to be her turn now!'

Do the kids treat them differently?

'Eric is very attached to Simone, Lisa maybe more to me. This happens in families.'

And we speak more about attachments and how these can shift, then like a scratched record I say again how unforgiveable I found it that Luisa did not want to meet Malú and her family that day in Florence, and it triggers something for me, because I feel my anger rising, and I tell Malú that Luisa's attitude to homosexuality was like her attitude to disability, to not acknowledge it, to look away, to simply pretend it didn't exist. How hard I find it to understand my mother's incapacity to have taken my daughter's epilepsy on board, or make allowances for her behaviour and accept her for who she was; for the pain I felt when she told me it was probably for the best that Rosa had died as she would be spared people's lack of sympathy and understanding in the future. How could she have thought that would make me feel better?

But Luisa is not completely intransigent, Malú reminds me. A year previously Luisa *did* briefly meet her children, after Malú persisted doggedly, offering to drop by whenever they happened to be in Florence.

Of course, how could I have forgotten? Malú had emailed to tell me. Now she elaborates.

'It was planned in advance. I told her we were coming and she agreed. I took them to her apartment. We only stayed about fifteen minutes. We had brought some pastries but they remained unopened because Luisa hadn't understood that they had been chosen by the kids for us to all eat together!' We both laugh. Typical.

'Luisa told the children some stories about the life she had lived. Lisa was quite interested, but Eric became bored and was having tantrums, throwing himself around. And then we left.'

I can picture the scene, the three of them climbing the ninety-three stairs to Luisa's apartment, then I see them enclosed in the dark book-lined sitting room, looking for somewhere to sit among the old newspapers and art catalogues piled high on every surface. I can imagine Lisa listening to Luisa's stories about the past but maybe wondering how long they have to stay, Eric getting restless and not keeping still, both longing for the package of pastries so carefully chosen to be opened; Luisa not thinking of doing so; Eric whispering loudly to his mother, 'what about the pastries?' and then, 'can we go now' and her shushing him and saying to Luisa, 'well, we must get going, it's been lovely to see you.'

Almost two hours have passed since Malú and I began talking. The hotel waiter who seemed so friendly at first is impatient when he comes in to clear our cups and plates, as if he is wondering how much longer we are intending to stay. I wonder if he has eavesdropped some of our conversation and is disapproving too. We get our things together to leave and realise that the piped music has stopped completely and that this 'library' only contains a handful of books.

At the station we order a quick espresso before we catch our separate trains: she back to Turin, me south, to Florence. There I will climb those endless stairs, ring the bell, kiss my mother hello and as I walk past a section of wall in her apartment where she keeps various notes, reminders and postcards received, something will catch my eye. Heavily written in a red coloured pencil I see Malú's address and her telephone numbers, traced several times over on a scrap of brown cardboard.

Later that evening as we eat supper in the kitchen that looks the same as it did in 1966, I mention in passing that I spent the day in Milan and had a 'nice cup of tea' with Malú, catching up. I follow that with a silent message that takes form in my head.

I'm so pleased you finally met her children.

But I leave it unvoiced.

I wish now I had said it out loud.

Pat

This is an open letter to a friend I cannot find. It is the only way I can think of communicating with her. It is also a way of exploring the landscape of youthful friendships and the perils of writing about them.

I last met Pat almost forty years ago and I already knew then that it was unlikely we would see each other again. I felt something close to resignation and relief in the sigh that accompanied the sound of the front door closing behind her, clicking shut on a relationship that was no longer working.

Pat rang the doorbell of my father's apartment that final time in the early summer of 1978. It was evening and I was tired, and when I saw her standing on the threshold with a boyfriend in tow my heart sank. Ben had died suddenly just weeks before, having collapsed in an Underground station after a night out with friends. I was busy sorting out a lot of things, grief-stricken and on edge.

She stood framed by the doorway, looking pale and scruffy, saying she needed somewhere to 'crash' in London with her friend.

'Look I'm sorry but this is a really bad time,' I said, explaining the situation. 'Things aren't going well, my father has died...'

I presume she said something sympathetic in response, but this was followed by: 'Can't we crash just tonight?'

Maybe I let them stay that night, maybe not. I know I didn't slam the door in their faces because I remember reluctantly letting them in. We stood around awkwardly in my room as she recounted the things they had been doing. Her hippie boyfriend hardly spoke. I felt detached and resentful, longing for them to leave.

After they had gone I decided to cut myself off from her. I didn't want to see her again.

When I think back to the early 1970s and my school friend Pat, I see a beautiful, clever but unconfident and self-destructive young woman, craving security and happiness but testing anybody willing to give either. It was as if she could not quite believe she could keep anything good, that it would not be taken away from her. In any case, more often than not what was on offer was anything but good. Unreliable men, particularly, would sense her vulnerability, her willingness to try things out, to please and adapt, and they would take advantage. It was the same for me at that time. We were two girls looking for affection, floundering in an age of unfettered sexual freedom.

A school photograph taken the summer before we began the sixth form shows me standing next to my American friend Ann, both of us with our 1970s middle-parted curtains of hair, hers fair and mine dark, giggling because a boy we considered a 'creep' – and who had confessed to a crush on me when I was even younger – had been placed next to me. Further along the row is Pat, big-boned and round-faced, with thick black hair covering one eye and shapeless clothes concealing her body. I can't remember exactly when or how she transformed into the slim, dark-haired Pre-Raphaelite beauty she became, the double of Jane Morris, muse to Dante Gabriel Rossetti – long limbs, aquiline nose, deep brown melancholic eyes, thick, lustrous hair. It must have been during the first year of the sixth form. As sixth-formers we hung out together a bit but I got to know her better the year after we left school, when I went to a tutorial college in Oxford to re-take some A levels. She was living with her parents and younger brother and sister on the outskirts of the city.

Our lives at that time were entwined in not always a positive way. Like me, she took risks, thinking that in doing so life would be more fun. The sense of humour we shared was of a dark kind, usually involving embarrassing situations we had put ourselves in. There was a destructive side to her nature that I identified with – it bonded us together.

The friendship was intense. We had a thing about 'adventures', dangerous hitchhiking trips that ended up in terrible scrapes. Once we found ourselves at the house of an African American air force man called Randy (we thought his name hilarious) who gave us so much strong grass to smoke that Pat became seriously paranoid and ill. I tried to hold on to her as she thrashed around on a big armchair, crying and shouting things I couldn't understand.

But that wasn't as bad as the time she took LSD. I had been too frightened to swallow the pill because I didn't trust my depressive mind and the demons it might unleash. I had just enough self-preservation left to know it would be a very bad idea. Not Pat.

In my sober state I was able to sit up with her all night as the drug took hold. She became extremely agitated, imagining spiders coming out of her skin, babies dying and other horrors. She felt all the torture and pain that the images evoked. I don't think this vision of hell put her off however, because she would hint at further experimentation and when I expressed concern her response was to laugh it off and imply that I was boring and unadventurous for not wanting to experiment myself. There was a sort of hierarchy of 'coolness' relating to the number and strength of drugs one consumed in the world we aspired to, but fear always prevented me from being too reckless.

A few years later, after Pat had been to see me at university, she wrote in a letter.

'Look, I didn't mean it when I said that about only getting on with people who tripped, it's just that I really need someone to straighten out my mind and a person who has tripped can tell me where the truths begin and the bullshit ends. That's all.'

As very young women we had been convinced that exposing ourselves to risk made us more interesting, and our lives more exciting, although much of what we got up to was just typical teenage behaviour. We smoked, drank, pilfered make-up, books and sweets; we gossiped and cringed about embarrassing things we had said or done. Both of us had tempestuous relationships with our mothers and academic fathers – I seem to remember hers was a physicist of some note.

Despite the volatility of our friendship, we were close. We understood and supported each other. When I wrote apologising that I had burdened her with my troubles the last time we had met, she answered, 'Don't talk a lot of crap! I'm just as fucked-up at the moment as you. Honestly, I'm going through hell. I can't explain it to anyone but you. When we're both down we do help each other because at least there's someone who understands, and if that doesn't make it better, it makes it bearable.'

Yes, I've preserved Pat's letters from all that time ago. I have them stored in a drawer along with the youthful journals and diaries I could never bring myself to throw away.

I've always kept notebooks to record thoughts, maybe because I can never trust myself to recall things correctly. While preoccupied with writing *Have You Been Good?* I carried one around in my bag until a bottle of water leaked and turned most of it into an inky blotch. But one sentence enclosed by quotation marks is still legible, although the source is not. Maybe it was simply an observation that was made to me.

'A memoir is *your* story, but of course it will involve many other people.'

I had taken the point to heart. I knew I must attempt to trace as many people from my past as possible. I owed it to them to inform them that they had been mentioned; that this was because they had made their mark on my life. It would be considerate to explain what I was doing and either warn them that I might be covering sensitive material or – where the relationship had been difficult – to ask whether they would prefer me to change their identity, even though in any case I was planning to use only their first names.

Initially I had been worried about how my immediate family might respond to my writing about them. My history was partly their history too. Fortunately their reaction was a positive one. My husband was supportive and even judged that a passage the editor suggested removing, describing my first impressions of his character in fair but unflattering terms, should be retained. My daughter Ellie's attitude was also 'do whatever you have to do'. I had been concerned that by giving so much emphasis to her sister and my grief over that terrible bereavement, it might unintentionally appear that I loved Ellie less. Over supper in a restaurant one evening I gave an emotional speech – at least *I* felt emotional – explaining that I had kept Ellie's presence in the background simply to protect her from exposure and to distance her from potential embarrassment. I told her how much she meant to me. 'I know, Mum, it's all right.' She smiled indulgently, and I could sense she was happy for me to change the subject. Later, when the book came out, she became my champion and supporter.

I turned my attention to my English cousins. This was more problematic because I wanted to write about my uncle Nigel and his wife Philippa with whom I had had a strained relationship during my childhood and young adulthood. Added to this was the fact that our common grandparents – Vita Sackville-West and Harold Nicolson – were in the public eye. My cousins might not appreciate the telling of my version, of how uncomfortable and unwelcome their parents made me feel in their family home. But they too were supportive. Adam lent me two large files of family papers that documented the difficult relationship his parents had with my mother Luisa, who kept forcing them to have me to stay after her divorce from my father. When I wrote about these strained 'holidays' at Sissinghurst Castle, I sent them extracts that included quotes from the correspondence between Luisa and their father. Adam wrote back acknowledging that Nigel had treated me badly; his sister Juliet answered separately: 'I am horrified by the insensitivity of both my parents and of how very, very little they understood about children...'

They said they understood, and that was reassuring.

There was one major problem. My mother. Our volatile relationship was central to my story but I knew she would not be happy with my recounting it. She has her own version of events and I knew she would not approve of me disclosing personal things for public consumption. So I tried to be as fair as possible, to tell it how it was for me. And when I came to the end of the book and did not feel strong enough to risk her fury and disapproval by showing it to her, I addressed her in the acknowledgements, writing that I hoped if she did come across the book, she would be able to forgive and understand myself and Rosa in our 'mad, sad and bad' entirety. To date I have not disclosed the book's existence to her; maybe I never shall. It is too difficult. She is in her mid-nineties and frail, and it is probably too late now anyway.

So that was family. I also wanted to write about past relationships. When contacted, two boyfriends from early on requested their names changed. One of them was kind and supportive, but understandably guarded. I suggested the name that had held a private meaning for us during our relationship. This was his emailed answer: 'I would very much appreciate and like that, as that is the person I was when I think of you and the person in me that I now treasure.' This made me wistful, as I had been very much in love with him. The other boyfriend communicated to me via his brother. That particular relationship had been a long and damaging one, and I was not surprised by the response. His brother wrote,

'I think the general feeling is that if it's a bit negative [the account of the relationship], it might be better if you changed his name.'

So I changed his name.

Steve, the only ex-boyfriend I had kept consistently in touch with (and the one I have devoted a chapter to in this collection) laughed and replied, 'Of course, use my real name! Any publicity is good publicity.' He was promoting his own creative project at the time.

There were other characters whose names I changed, for example the girl who bullied me at school. I couldn't face getting in touch after finding her photograph on a website. I was pleased to see she was doing good things with her life after surviving difficult experiences, but the sight of the same hard mouth and beady eyes in adult form made me feel like a nervous ten-year-old again.

Some friends proved difficult to find. I wrote to ex-work and home addresses, I called old telephone numbers, I searched on Google and social media sites. A school friend, Lydia (another subject in this collection of stories), had materialised a couple of years previously, found through contacting her brother's workplace.

And then I came to Pat. Unlike Lydia, she had a popular surname that made her harder to trace. Mutual friends had lost touch with her. Google came up with so many people with the same name who clearly were not her. Social media proved the same. I contacted our school to see if she appeared in the list of alumni. The secretary wrote back, 'Unfortunately we have no details of Pat **** in our records.'

I had retained her name in my memoir as I did with other friends who made an appearance and whom I had not been able to find. Should I have changed everyone's name? At the time I felt not, as if by doing so the authenticity of the book would be compromised.

An early draft of my memoir had included several anecdotes about my escapades with Pat. By our late teens things were going wrong between us. For a while an unhealthy element of competition had begun creeping into our friendship: who was more depressed, who had the most drama in their lives, which of us had survived the most embarrassing situations (or 'cringes' as we referred to them). Everything was processed through this spectrum of negativity and competition.

'When you phoned me up and told me your cringe in London, I thought, oh poor Nessa, why does it always seem to happen to her! Well, from now on I'm going to reserve all sympathy for myself...' she wrote, followed by a detailed description of a sequence of humiliations with an object of desire over an eventful weekend.

The empathy we had for each other was beginning to transmute into a scoring of points. And then came the flirting with my boyfriends.

The summer after we had taken our A levels I met Peter, a young reporter on the local newspaper. I had been having a drink with a friend in a pub in Notting Hill, close to my father's flat, and Peter was sitting on his own at the table next to ours. We struck up a conversation that led to his arranging to meet me the following weekend. I liked him, he was attractive and bright, and I was impressed that being slightly older, he had a job. Not any old job, but a job that involved writing.

Even though it turned out that there was not that much of a spark between us, I felt a twinge of apprehension when I introduced him to Pat a short while later. She began blatantly flirting and sure enough within the week he had transferred his affections to her. Although their association didn't last long either, she still told me later on that she had asked him which one of us was better in bed. 'Oh God, I don't want to know!' I shouted as Pat tried to tell me anyway.

I never mentioned Peter in my memoir. But I wrote about Leon, the boyfriend who followed soon after. I wrote about him because he made me pregnant just before he also went off with Pat. I had not thought of this as a 'betrayal' because I didn't particularly care about him either as I was still in love with my school boyfriend, whom I believed had rejected me.

The three of us all continued being friends, in fact Pat and I would even laugh together about Leon's idiosyncrasies (his habit of scratching his chest while talking, for example). It was in Pat's parents' house that I miscarried, and one of the things I remembered vividly and described in my book was the fact that she had become anxious about me soiling her mother's towels in the process. We were both terrified of our mothers.

After that miscarriage I returned to my father in London and sunk into deep despondency. I didn't want to see Pat for a while.

Things were not going so well for her with Leon either, and we were both spiralling down into depression. Clearly neither of us was strong enough to support each other. I desperately needed direction. As did she, but I had not the resources to help her.

The prescription the doctor gave me to feel better only made me worse. In the end I realised the only person who could help was myself. I took myself off the pills and went to Italy – first to my mother in Florence and then on a trip to Sicily and Malta with my father, who was doing research for a book on the followers of Caravaggio. When I got back to London there were two letters waiting for me. One was from another school friend of ours, Cherry, with whom I had lived in Oxford, telling me that Pat had also suffered a miscarriage. I couldn't believe it, it was incredible – she had been admitted to the same hospital that patched me up just weeks before. 'She was in the same ward, even' – Cherry underlined the sentence for emphasis – 'in the same bed.' Worse than that, Cherry wrote, Pat also had an infection in her fallopian tubes. 'It makes me think,' Cherry continued, 'that maybe there is something wrong with Leon?'

The second letter was from Pat, telling me what had happened. 'Apparently I've got an infection in my fallopian tubes. Drag! Otherwise they think I've had a miscarriage.'

I answered, expressing sympathy. Her next letter ended: 'Come straight round to Oxford when you get back.'

I did go and see her, and she asked me to stay with her for a while. We had discussed all sharing a place together, she, Leon and I, but their liaison had become shaky and all in all it seemed a bad idea. Still, I had no plans. Pat's parents said I could have a room in their house as long as Pat and I made an effort to get some work.

So I stayed in Oxford. Leon had gone, and Pat and I got jobs waitressing in Oxford's smartest hotel, situated next to the main theatre. Once I served the rock band Queen; she got to wait on David Bowie. I applied to some universities and got a place to start the following September. Finally I felt as if I had some focus.

Living and working with Pat didn't work out, however. Peggy, the manager of the hotel restaurant, didn't like the fact that our giggling and gossiping got in the way of our work, so she gave us different shifts. We hardly saw one another, and when we did, we were tired and got on each other's nerves. I felt uneasy staying at her parents' house when she wasn't there, especially as Pat's relationship with her mother was so volatile. In any case, within a month I had been dismissed by Peggy for clumsily pouring soup into the lap of the politician Willie Whitelaw. Pat meanwhile had gone off with a group of musicians she had met in the restaurant – the support band to David Essex, teen idol of the time.

I was aimless again, sleeping at Ben's flat in London, or visiting old school friends. I would get enthusiastic about an idea – joining a kibbutz in Israel or travelling to the US, and then sink into defeated apathy at the first hurdle.

Pat too was having a difficult time. With Leon gone from both our lives, we eventually each got new boyfriends and went our separate ways: I to university, she to something resembling a commune (or so it seemed in the context of its time), but we kept in touch through letters and did visit each other on a couple of occasions.

'How glad I feel that I finally got down to Brighton and saw you in your natural habitat,' she wrote after a visit to my student house. I still have a postcard she sent me in 1977, while in my second year at university. 'Hello slagheap, this is Patric… Guess who I just bumped into? Leon! Hasn't changed much – but no chest scratching thank God – with this poor nice girl too! Nuff nastiness…'

She made me laugh sometimes, but I was wary, because our friendship could be so destructive. Which is why, when the doorbell of my father's flat rang that late spring evening in 1978 and I found her standing on the threshold with a hippie boyfriend in tow, my heart sank.

Three of the old photographic portraits chosen to illustrate my book depict the person slightly obscured. This was intentional, to retain an element of anonymity. Remi at school caught running out of the sixth form study we used to share. Paul's long hair flowing, walking with me in the mid-1970s along the Holland Park street Ben lived in, our arms linked, me turning my head back to the camera and smiling, him looking ahead, away from the third, anonymous figure who is taking the picture (who could that have been?). And Pat in the long cape I remember well, her hair covering most of her face, talking to me by the large cedar tree in our school's grounds.

One of the effects of publishing my memoir was that friends and acquaintances from my past got in touch. I had mentioned the name of my house in the book, so it was easy for them to address their letters to me there. Former colleagues of my father, childhood friends, even my nursery teacher who on a postcard wrote, 'I remember you vividly as a wide-eyed, serious little girl… I have one recollection of the time you got a tiny glass bead stuck up your nose and had to sniff pepper to successfully sneeze it out.'

So it was with a smile that one day I recognised Pat's distinctive looped handwriting on the envelope pushed through the letterbox by the postman. My old friend had got in touch – she must have come across my memoir too!

I opened her letter impatiently and with enthusiasm. Inside were three pages of black biro on white lined paper, as if torn from a student notepad. As I read it I found myself responding to parts as if we were having a conversation, my thoughts interjecting with questions and comments.

The letter began sympathetically.

'Dear Vanessa, I was very sorry to read of your painful loss, and having gone through similar experiences myself, I feel deeply for you, and wish you well in the future.'

Oh no, have you too lost a child?

'However, I must make an interjection here: as regarding the matter of Leon. My recollection is that you were a tad unimpressed by him and proffered the thought to pass him off to me: an amusing interlude, between two slightly immature friends.'

That's right. Yes I certainly was 'a tad unimpressed'!

'I do however apologise for "losing it" over my mother's bed linen but, as my mother is as fearsome as yours appears to be, I can understand my panic. But this does not condone my insensitivity. I apologise again.'

No need to.

'Obviously, it was a painful experience for both of us – as I had a miscarriage also from the torrid…'

'Torrid' or 'horrid'? I frown, peering at this word I cannot decipher.

'…experiment.'

So it was definitely a miscarriage, not an infection in your fallopian tubes? But hang on, what do you mean, 'experiment'? He just went from me to you, and it didn't bother me. 'Experiment'?

'Your hurtful rejection of me is at last explained, but I suggest there was also a lot of ego involved, and since we discussed the possibility of a *ménage à trois* beforehand…'

I hadn't meant in that way, Pat!

'I cannot accept full responsibility for all your hurt…'

I wasn't hurt about that; Leon had nothing to do with my cutting ties with you. That happened four years later, after my father's death…

'Anyway – water under the bridge – we must all move on, and your behaviour is at last explained.'

But Pat, we exchanged friendly letters and met up a few times well after Leon had disappeared…

'If it helps you at all, your "waking dream" of your dear daughter…'

(This must refer to the beginning of my memoir when I write of 'seeing' my daughter getting on a bus nine months after her death. I end the passage, 'I have become insane, I think. With the loss of her I have lost part of myself.')

'… does not preclude insanity.'

What? Are you are suggesting my insanity should not be ruled out?

'It is a common enough experience – and spiritual in essence. So do not worry yourself on that account.'

Oh, are you using the word 'preclude' incorrectly?

'Over time your feelings for your daughter will distil into a deep expression of being given the opportunity of deep love, and that is a great honour. I wish your family well, Regards, Pat.'

I kept hold of the letter in my hand long after I had finished reading it. I was formulating my response. So desperately did I want to put my case forward: to make her see and understand. But no contact details were included.

'Let it go,' advised my friends, 'why do you care so much?'

'Because she's got it wrong! I need to tell her, I need to put it right, she must acknowledge the truth.'

Pat had given no address, email, or telephone number. And so I set to work again, trying to find her, as I had when I first began writing my memoir. Back to Facebook, Google, our old school, the friends we had had in common. Surely someone must know where she is?

Nothing. No one.

I brought out her old letters and found the same telephone number scribbled in the corner of one or two of them. I keyed in the number with a fluttering heart. What if by chance she should still live there, and pick up? What exactly was I going to say?

'The number you have dialled has not been recognised. Please check and try again.'

All I had left to go on was the clear postmark: 'Swindon'. I looked up directory enquiries for the area but her surname was so common, there was no illuminating information to be had. Pat had a younger sister and brother; I couldn't remember the boy's name but put Naomi's into Google. Again nothing came up.

And so I'm giving up the quest. If you should ever see this, Pat, wherever you are, you may well feel further aggrieved. Somehow my hope is you can appreciate that it is the only way left for me to communicate.

My archive is my alibi. The letters and cards we exchanged in the few years after that episode are testament to the fact that there were no hard feelings around Leon. It certainly was not because of him that I withdrew from my relationship with you. But I was developing into a different person and when I closed the door to you after Ben's death I was vulnerable and needed to protect myself. The power games within our friendship were getting tired.

* * *

So is it all about power, or simply a question of conflicting individual truth? Are we back to Delacroix's observation that our imagination contributes to the picture, that all memory is reconstructed? Do I have the upper hand now, by publishing? Maybe power games are at work in any friendship, as are misunderstandings, self-deception and bad faith. But equally in withholding her address, so I cannot reply, Pat holds some power too. Have we found a point of balance now?

A Pre-Raphaelite Pat: *Mrs William Morris in a Blue Silk Dress* by Dante Gabriel Rossetti

The story does not end there. By a strange coincidence, shortly after I complete this collection of stories, a letter arrives from a reader, a stranger, telling me he has just finished my memoir. He continues:

> I'm writing to you now – after some thought – because for 15 years or so I was married to your friend Pat. She spoke of you from time

> to time and so of course when I realised you had written about your life and about your school, I was more than usually interested.
>
> I think she was always disappointed that you and she lost touch. I never learned why, though I expect you may have had good reason for ending the friendship. Pat and I separated about 10 years ago, though we have a son who is now 28 and who we both see fairly regularly. So as I said, I thought about this for a while but eventually decided it would be unkind not to see if you were both interested in getting back in touch. If you would like her contact details, please reply to this letter and I will see if she would welcome an approach – or maybe I could just pass on an email address?

He fortunately includes all his contact details and I respond immediately, informing him of Pat's recent letter, attaching my 'Pat' story, asking him for more details about what has happened to her in the intervening years. He emails back, and I learn that she suffered a terrible loss by suicide, not of her own child, but no less tragic for that. She has now reached a degree of peace through embracing a set of unconventional beliefs and this, he explains, has become her truth.

'Sadly, I don't think you can fix anything,' he adds. 'In my experience she will not acknowledge your truth. Even if you persuade her of it on one day, tomorrow she will have reconstructed the narrative, and your truth will be lost.'

His offer of passing on 'an approach' has got me thinking. Here is my opportunity. I can now get in touch directly and explain things. I can clarify. I can get some resolution, some reparation. I spent so much time and effort in trying to find her, and this opportunity has now been handed to me on a plate. Yet I dither and frown – communication will be difficult, impossible even, why push this further? I convince myself she will be unable to understand, it will make matters worse.

And so I withdraw, and in doing so feel a strange sense of unease, mixed with relief.

Lydia

There is a town in Spain, deep in its balmy south, where Goya once sketched young and old alike. One night I meet Lydia and Tom there, in a bar looking across to a natural park of pine trees on the dunes and the village of Almonte, home to the Virgin of El Rocio. The statue of the 'Madonna of the Dew' has been worshipped since the thirteenth century, and is brought, once a year, across the water by boat. It is the final day of the festival, and pilgrims have come in brightly painted wagons from across the region. There is a party atmosphere, with numerous families dressed in Andalusian costume: broad-brimmed hats and short trousers for men, flouncy flamenco dresses for women. The proud, stiff-backed poses of the young women echo Goya's drawings, made in this very place over two hundred years ago.

This evening Tom drinks beer while Lydia and I prefer whisky to the local manzanilla. I feel a twinge of envy for the happy, extended family groups – mothers, fathers, grandmothers, children – and as Lydia talks about her daughter Nessie, I am moved, and my eyes fill with tears. She notices, reaches across the table and squeezes my hand. 'But look,' she says, smiling, 'here we are in this lovely place. Our losses have brought us together. And we must be happy for that.'

I had come to Spain to see Lydia and speak with her about resilience. Despite all the misfortunes she has experienced, her capacity to adjust and recover is astounding, as well as inspirational. Optimism is her default position. When I first asked if I could write her story she emailed back a question.

'Where should I start?'

Begin at the beginning.

'As a child I was always so determined to be happy. I even asked my mother to change my name to "Happy". When she told me that she couldn't do that, I cried and she said, "You see, you can't always be happy."' Her mother was to be proved right many times over.

Among my school friends Lydia was my father's favourite. They shared a sense of life's absurdities, and in her company he would laugh like a schoolboy. At one point in the early 1970s Lydia was homeless and Ben offered to put her up in his spare bedroom in return for doing the washing up. Even when she vanished for days and the dishes piled up, he didn't complain. A few weeks before I started university he paid for her to come on holiday with us to Crete. Within days she had hooked up with Nikos, a waiter at Hotel Grammatikakis, leaving me sulky about losing my companion for long stretches of time. Ben's friend Ginette had come too, and as we sat wondering if Lydia was going to join us for lunch or not, she gave vent to some of her irritation. But Ben would not hear a word said against her.

Forty years later, in southern Spain where Lydia now lives, she shows me the hotel brochure she kept as a souvenir. We laugh at the bikini-clad lovelies and their boyfriends clothed only in tightly fitting swimming trunks, posing in the hotel grounds and on the adjoining beach. In fact what I remember most from that holiday is how much my nineteen-year-old self wished I could join the hippies sleeping under the stars rather than return to my comfortable hotel bedroom.

'I adored Ben,' Lydia says, 'and I loved that holiday.'

Apart from once accompanying Ben and Ginette on a trip to Knossos, we would wave them off when they went sightseeing, happy to spend the day on the beach.

Lydia laughs. 'Do you remember when Ben put on his swimming trunks and laid down spread-eagled on the sand and said, "I suppose this is what you do to sunbathe?"'

Yes! My unworldly father had never heard of sunbathing until we said we planned to do a lot of it. Lydia continues, 'And I loved going down to the bar and having an ouzo with him in the morning.'

An ouzo in the morning? I don't believe I joined in on that.

Lydia arrived at our hippie school for the summer term of the sixth form dressed in a blue suede mini skirt, soon exchanged for our 'uniform' of jeans, T-shirt and bare feet. The reason for her Catholic parents' unlikely decision to send her to the extremely liberal Frensham Heights was the reluctance of other (possibly better) schools to enrol her after she had been expelled from two convents in succession. She was bright, with a good academic record, but the happy, stable child had turned into a rebellious teenager.

The first convent expelled her after the nuns intercepted sexually suggestive letters from a young friend called Stephen. The headmistress of the second convent cut her more slack but Lydia was finally dismissed for stealing the paschal candle and communion wine during the power cuts – frequent in the early 1970s – and holding a party in her room. Her parents, based in Johannesburg where her father was British Consul, were summoned by telegram to remove their wayward daughter. Lydia's mother flew to Britain to find another school willing to take her on and Frensham Heights was the only one to oblige at such short notice.

Lydia drew attention from the moment she arrived. She was an engaging, tomboyish girl with a ready smile and she made friends easily, getting on equally well with boys and girls. Her thick, brown, curly hair framed a freckly, feline face and when she smiled her nose crinkled prettily. In my memory she was always laughing and getting into scrapes. She certainly liked provoking authority. One holiday from school she borrowed a T-shirt of mine that featured Jimi Hendrix's head on the front, and immediately got stopped and searched at Johannesburg airport, entering apartheid-era South Africa. Lydia told me crazy stories of her father's experiences as British Consul there, such as the time some holidaymakers asked him to get them returned to Britain as soon as possible because they hadn't realised there would be quite so many black people in South Africa. 'You're joking?' I would say, open-mouthed.

She flourished at our liberal school. Because she was naturally intelligent, she did well in exams without putting in much effort, and her sunny nature drew people to her. It was as if she trusted that others would like her, and that events would turn out well. When she hitchhiked, as many of us did at that time, she met interesting characters – including the gorgeous Simon, a twenty-three-year-old who lived close to the school and became her boyfriend for a while – whereas I, tending towards melancholy, projected a certain vulnerability that seemed to attract every damaged and exploitative man in the vicinity.

Lydia's optimism enabled situations to become joyful and she carried me in her slipstream, jollying me along when I began sinking into gloom, giving me a sense of stability and care that I lacked at home.

Her father was transferred to the consulate in Seville and so it was to Spain that Lydia returned when we left school. Here she met Paco Tejero, a working-class boy employed to do odd jobs in her parents' flat. Despite having had to leave school aged fourteen to earn money for his family, he attracted Lydia with his knowledge of poetry and his hatred for the Franco regime.

She was bored in Spain, though, and returned to England, living with her uncle in west London, and as she puts it, 'trying desperately to conform.' She wrote to me in November 1973, and I still have the letter.

'My plans are quite complicated. Don't criticise, I honestly know what I'm doing. I've refused both universities and decided on a bilingual secretarial course in French, English and Spanish. Now for explanations – I'm probably getting married in September. Don't frown! I need to be earning good money and I need to be able to get jobs and work permits easily. I wish I could talk to you because I don't think you would understand this written, I will explain but please meanwhile understand.'

She knew I would disapprove. Choosing to be someone's secretary *and* get married! The two things my friends and I most looked down upon – to train for a job that would make you shackled to men (as bosses in 1973 were usually men) and to be married, like old people! It felt as if I had lost her.

I bring this up when we meet, all these years later, and refer to that letter. 'You were such a bright, sassy girl, and for you to disappear and become a housewife in Spain seemed an unbearable thing…'

'Yeah, yeah,' laughs Lydia, 'and it was!'

Finding languages easy, she began not a 'bi' but a 'tri'lingual secretarial course – French, English, Spanish – and worked shifts at a local pub in the evenings to make some money. The bar work proved more fun than the course and when she was offered extra lunchtime slots, she couldn't resist the temptation to skip lessons. The secretarial training was soon abandoned altogether and she began working and living in the pub with the couple that ran it. They became her second family. I was living in London then, and I would take the Underground to Ealing to spend evenings sitting at the bar while she pulled pints and chatted with the regulars. She was popular and seemed contented.

That all changed when the owners of the pub left and Lydia no longer had a home. She wanted to be independent, so was reluctant to return to her uncle's house.

'I decided to explore the lives of the homeless, went to the soup kitchens and even camped in the park with the alcoholics whom I already knew from the pub.'

That too I recall, a sunny afternoon in a run-down park, drinking cider and smoking cheap cigarettes with her down-at-heel friends, going home and mentioning it to Ben. I think it was then that he offered her the spare bedroom in his flat in exchange for doing the washing up.

Her lifestyle began taking its toll. Still only a teenager, she was tired and directionless.

'I think my mother guessed that I was in a bad way and came back to save me. We looked at the newspapers together and found a job at the London Tourist Board which sounded interesting. She took me clothes shopping to buy a new dress and I went for the interview and got the job. I loved it and made several interesting friends.'

But Paco was still in the background waiting to make her his wife. She returned to Seville on holiday to be married and together they came back to England.

'Big mistake!' Lydia then glosses over what must have been a devastating realisation about her new husband. 'After a few days of marriage, I had a black eye over a stupid row.' I press her further on this, but she can't remember what the argument was about.

Life carried on. Within a few months she was pregnant and Paco told her that he should be the money earner and they should return to Seville, so she left the London job and the friends she loved and returned with him to Spain.

When her son David was a year old, she found a job as PA to the director of an olive exporting firm and her life changed drastically. From being stuck at home with a bully of a husband and a young baby, she found herself surrounded by new friends, and once she was promoted to a managerial position, she was doing work she really enjoyed. She began an affair with a colleague and they became inseparable. 'We went everywhere together as soulmates do. He was amusing and we were on the same wavelength. However, we were discreet about our physical relationship.'

After nine months, her double life became too stressful, and she returned to England with Paco and David, determined to make a fresh start. Over the previous years she and I hadn't been in touch much, but she came to visit me at the home in north London I was sharing with my then-boyfriend Steve. It was the winter of 1981. Lydia arrived with her little boy in tow, and we sat rather self-consciously in the sitting room, drinking tea. Our lives seemed worlds apart. She had a child and responsibilities. I was working as a researcher in the BBC picture library and the idea of marriage and children were the furthest things from my mind. I can't remember her telling me anything about her strained marriage or the man she was having an affair with. We chatted rather blandly, laughed along with her small son and said goodbye with a hug.

I lost touch with her for almost thirty years.

It was around Christmas time in 2008 and I was talking to another old school friend, Tessa, about grief. In July of that year my nineteen-year-old daughter Rosa had drowned, having suffered an epileptic fit while swimming. Tessa was looking thoughtful. 'You know, something has just come back to me. A few years ago I saw a report in a local newspaper about a terrible car accident. The two young girls in the back of the car were killed instantly. I remember being struck by the girl's name – Vanessa Tejero – and that of the mother quoted in the article, Lydia Biggie...'

'You don't think...? I know she had a son, I don't know about a daughter...'

We set to work. We contacted the *Evening Argus*, the local newspaper that had reported the accident. Yes, they had a record of that story but they did not have any contact details. We searched Lydia's name on the Internet. Nothing came up under her maiden or married name. She was one of six siblings, surely one of them could be traced?

Jane, Ben, Sara and Hugh.

Nothing.

The other brother?

Louis.

And then up it came, 'Louis Biggie, Director of Learning Solutions', Johns Hopkins University, Baltimore. In seconds I was on the university website and there was his email address.

'This is a long shot but are you Lydia's brother?'

Louis responded instantly.

'Lydia would love to hear from you. She is living in Spain now. I know that you were her very, very special friend and that she has been sad not to be in touch with you.'

A few months later, in March 2009, Tessa and I were walking through the arrivals hall at Gibraltar airport. Lydia was going to pick us up but I couldn't see her among the assembled people meeting passengers off the plane.

'I think that's her,' whispered Tessa, and I looked again at the middle-aged woman in a fleece, standing in the crowd with a little dog by her side, waving and smiling enthusiastically. It took me a moment to readjust – as if my eyesight was faulty – and start to reconfigure Lydia from young to middle-aged. It was only after I recognised her way of speaking, and her habit of laughing at the end of each sentence, that my old school friend came into focus again and any awkwardness was gone.

Lydia was living in a small apartment with her partner, Tom, in Zahara de los Atunes, a Spanish town situated next to a long stretch of Atlantic beach. She had found cheap off-season holiday accommodation for Tessa and I to share for a few days. That evening she cooked a typically English meal of shepherd's pie – was there also a fruit crumble? – and we reminisced, no doubt boring Tom with our stories about school and old friends. When I had to pass her bedroom to get to the bathroom, I noticed a framed photograph of a young teenage girl, propped on the bedside table. 'Was that Vanessa?' I asked on my return to the kitchen. She nodded, 'yes', but didn't go in to details then. It was Mother's Day, and perhaps we were both feeling fragile.

We kept in touch after that, and I learnt more about what had happened between our meeting as young women in the early 1980s, and my trip to Spain in 2009. When I asked her permission to write her 'back story', she filled in the gaps, partly in emailed responses, partly when we met up again more recently.

Missing her job, and with Spanish-speaking Paco needing to find work, the couple had returned with their little son to Spain. Lydia was readmitted to her job and life continued as before. Unfortunately, after eleven years, the factory was taken over by another large multinational and amalgamated with the biggest olive exporting firm in Spain. Lydia had six months to decide whether to accept a pay-off and leave, or stay on. She decided to leave.

Her daughter Vanessa had been born in December 1985 and was three years old. Lydia was looking forward to being more of a 'hands-on' mum. But she hadn't taken into account that she would be back at home with the bully, and she became deeply unhappy as the marriage became more strained. The problem was Paco's fluctuating moods. He was well liked by their community and if they were out in the street he might laugh and tell jokes with the neighbours, but inside the home he was sullen, critical, unpredictable. Lydia might try to please him by placing a beautifully cooked meal in front of him, but he would only find fault. 'He would say it was too hot or something. He never appreciated anything.'

By 1992, Lydia had decided she had enough. She set off with an agreed 100,000 pesetas settlement and her little girl Nessie, leaving her son David, aged fourteen, behind in Seville. That must have been hard. 'Well, his mind had been poisoned against me by his father,' Lydia says. When, in her own words, she 'had gone off the rails' by going out all the time with her friends and continuing her affair with her colleague, Paco would track her down, David in tow, and point out her 'bad mother' deficiencies to their son.

So leaving her teenage son behind, Lydia and her six-year-old daughter set off in her Renault 5 up to Santander to catch the ferry to Plymouth with the car loaded to the hilt with all their possessions. She parked near the port and waited till dawn to drive on to the ferry. Nessie was comfortably installed in the car, wrapped in the duvet on top of the luggage, and Lydia managed to snatch a little sleep during a long night. When they arrived in Plymouth they drove straight to her parents – now retired – in Chichester, and began trying to sort out their lives.

First, Lydia went to the employment office and applied for housing benefit. Unfortunately, this was denied as she had declared that she was the legal owner of a property in Spain. After much persuasion and explanations that she had no financial backing, her parents were not well off, and she could not sell her flat as her ex-husband and son were living there, she was granted both housing benefit and income support and managed to rent a comfortable flat a short walk from an infant school for Nessie. She decided that her best course of action, with such a young child, was to go to a women returner's course and get a qualification in computing.

But Nessie was badly affected by the move and homesick for Spain. At Christmas Lydia relented and decided to go back for a couple of weeks, mainly to see whether her daughter would realise that returning wasn't the best way forward. 'Coming back to England was painful. Nessie wasn't really happy and the theme continued throughout the year even though she enjoyed her new friends and, on the surface, seemed happy.'

When the summer holidays came round, Lydia came to a decision and drove to Seville with Nessie in an empty car to see whether there might be any available work. A tennis club offered her the job of looking after four teenage tennis players and organising tournaments in exchange for a low wage, board and lodging. She drove back to England on her own leaving Nessie safe and happy with Paco, David and her friends to collect all their things.

It turned out to be no more than a nanny / cook position for four difficult teenagers. Money was short and she had to do her best to provide them with the three-course lunches and suppers they expected. She would hang around the front door of the apartment in the hope that the man who had employed her would turn up with enough cash to buy the bread they expected to accompany their meal. The accommodation given to them was a small, dingy inside room overlooking a lift well.

There was another surprise in store. One day seven-year-old Nessie unexpectedly said she wished they were back in England. When Lydia tentatively asked her why, Nessie answered that she had been happier there except that she didn't like Sally, a family friend they had been staying with. When Lydia probed further, Nessie revealed that it wasn't Sally she was against but Sally's husband.

Lydia froze. She had heard rumours that he had been accused of physically abusing his own three-year-old daughter but, at the time, refused to believe it. And now could he have possibly done the same to Nessie? She kept her cool and persuaded the child to tell her what had happened.

'Nessie told me that while he was rocking her on his lap, he'd touched her up. I was so relieved to hear that she had still had her pants on but it shook me to the core.'

After their return to England, Lydia went with her brother Hugh to report this to social services. They knew that social services were aware of the family, and felt a responsibility to register their concerns. But the response was that Sally and her husband were getting on well now and the family unit should not be disrupted or 'spoilt'. What about Sally's own abused child? The case against the father had been dropped as it was thought it would be too traumatic to put such a young child through the courts.

A few years later the man moved in with another family and Lydia read in the local paper that he had been charged for abuse within that family. She never learnt whether he was actually arrested.

Lydia left the 'tennis teenagers' work and went back with Nessie to Paco's flat, sleeping on the sofa and wondering what to do next. Her son David was still behaving in a cold and antagonistic way towards her so she decided to return to England with Nessie. This time she trained in IT and got a job with a medical insurance firm. Nessie went to primary school, made new friends and renewed her relationship with her infant school friends. Life was good. They were on a small budget but gradually Lydia got promoted, and Nessie started secondary school where she was a popular, sociable child. With the support of a new partner, Ant, Lydia bought a house, and he moved in with them.

Nessie wasn't too keen on Ant but they decided to make an effort to get on with one another. During the summer of 1999, while Nessie was on holiday in Spain, Lydia and Ant travelled out to Portugal for a month-long holiday. They had a wonderful time and Ant and she decided they should live there and that Nessie, who had continued to insist she missed living abroad, could do so too by returning to live with her father and brother.

But thirteen-year-old Nessie no longer wanted to leave the UK. She reluctantly agreed to the plan but insisted that her last few months in England should be spent enjoying herself. She spent weekends either at home with friends or sleeping at her friends' homes, as if she wished to stock up memories she could draw on later.

On 6 November 1999, about a month before her fourteenth birthday, Nessie had gone to stay with her friend Terrina, together with Dionne, a close school friend. She telephoned at 5.06 p.m. – Lydia remembers the exact time – to say that they were fine and were going out but had to do a few things before leaving.

Lydia fills in the details.

'She rang off after saying, "love you!" and I went back to the sofa to watch Heartbeat with Ant. Shortly after seven o'clock, the doorbell rang. Two police officers were on the doorstep, one male, one female. They asked if I was Vanessa Tejero's mother and I said yes. One of them said, "Your daughter's been in an accident and hasn't survived." I felt frozen to the spot. Ant ran around the room saying, "Fuck, fuck" and I didn't know what to do. The woman asked me whether I wanted to call anyone and I said I wanted to speak to my brother Hugh. I phoned him and hysterically gave him the news and all he could say was, "Where's Lydia?"'

A recently qualified seventeen-year-old boy had been driving at breakneck speed and lost control on a bend and another car had crashed into them. The boy and Terrina survived, but Nessie and Dionne were killed instantly. Lydia had to go to the hospital to identify the body, the same hospital where her father had been admitted the week before, and where he died two weeks later. Lydia's mother had died only the previous year.

So much loss. But Lydia says simply, 'I was lucky. My optimistic view on life helped me through and, with the help of family and friends, I gradually improved.'

She was repeatedly challenged to draw on that inner strength. 'They performed an autopsy and then summoned us to the hospital to view "the bodies" again. The coroner said they'd first show us Nessie but got it wrong and showed us Dionne.'

'They took you to the wrong body? How could they?'

I am appalled.

'It distressed me so much. When he showed us Nessie, her face looked far more damaged than after the first viewing and that upset me again.'

Lydia hoped to bury Nessie in England but Paco wanted her in Spain. She knew the cemetery in Seville and had demanded that Nessie should be cremated if she was to be returned to Spain. Paco swore he would do so but a few years later confessed that he had gone back on his word and had buried her in the cemetery. Lydia has never visited her grave.

Misfortune continued to pursue her, despite periods of stability and happiness in between. 'Life with Ant was never easy', she says. 'It was never boring either and we had great fun together. However much we loved one another, he had fits of temper which were always followed by profuse apologies. Money was tight until he managed to close an ongoing court case and we were suddenly better off. We bought a beautiful, traditional Portuguese house on the clifftops in Maria Vinagre and started travelling around Europe, leaving a friend to look after the house.'

In November 2002, Lydia woke up to find Ant sitting on the sofa complaining of terrible heartburn. She tried, with no success, to get him to see the doctor. By the time he got to hospital the news was not good. He had suffered a heart attack and had a leaking valve that could only be operated on in Lisbon. For the next seven weeks Lydia stayed in a hotel near the hospital.

After three open-heart operations Ant seemed to improve, but one night she was woken by a phone call at two in the morning.

'It was very unusual for him to wake me during the night. He asked if I was OK and I asked him the same. He reassured me but, when I woke at six, I sensed something was wrong and rushed to the hospital, went up to his room and was told that he was back in intensive care. I raced upstairs and was told that they were trying to stabilise him. At seven o'clock, the doctor came out to tell me that he'd died. I could hardly believe it. We had plans to be married in May.'

As if things couldn't get worse, Ant's thirty-year-old daughter who Lydia had treated as her own, took her to court, demanding an out of court settlement of £25,000, which Lydia did not have to give. The trial, when it came round, lasted three days. Lydia had gathered her own evidence to disprove the affidavits brought against her, and both she and her lawyer agreed that they had a very good case in their favour. But the judge did not take her side. She lost everything and was faced with high legal costs.

Lydia went to live in a place called Jimena where she was shown kindness and support by old friends of Ant. She began helping out a couple, a Norwegian man called Tom and his wife Anna, who ran a holiday-let in the village. Unfortunately Anna had mental health problems and, shortly after the New Year, was taken into the nearby psychiatric home where she spent the next three months. After she was discharged, Anna's behaviour became increasingly unpredictable, once even kidnapping Lydia's little dog Tinker. She threw Tom out of their home three times, and finally Tom went to live with Lydia.

He and Lydia have been together ever since. After I saw them in 2009, Lydia inherited money from her uncle, and they have moved from the apartment in Zahara to a house on the outskirts of a town called Sanlúcar de Barrameda. She has made her peace with her son David, and is the loving grandmother of his two small children.

It is here in Sanlúcar that I ask: where does her resilience and optimism come from? I wonder if her Catholic upbringing gave her strength. Is it simply a sense of faith that gives her comfort and the feeling that life must go on, no matter what?

She answers that she wasn't a 'good Catholic' although she was brought up to go to church. Rather than Catholicism, she attributes the strong bonds in her family as the foundation of her strength and security, and the result of that secure base is what she refers to as her optimism. And yet optimism is a faith of sorts, is it not, for everyone? A belief that things will improve, a drive to enjoying life as best we can – the hope that the future can offer better things and that nothing bad is final.

'Any religious faith I might have had just evaporated after what happened to me,' she says, referring to her daughter's death. 'But surprisingly, I was always positive that it wasn't the last time I had seen Nessie. And that must be something to do with religious faith.'

Steve

I think he would like to be called Stephen now, but he will always remain Steve to me. Bouncy, gregarious and enthusiastic, but with a darker, troubled side I only learnt of later when I got to know him better. We became friends as our time at Sussex University was coming to an end and when he went to work in Paris for an advertising agency we kept in touch. Over Easter in 1980, I broke a train journey to Italy to visit him, and our relationship developed into something more serious. By autumn he had left Paris and was living with me in London, and the following spring he suggested a trip to Israel to stay with his brother and family in Jerusalem.

Before that trip, the fact that he was Jewish and I was not had seemed an irrelevance – just a statement of fact. But I was hurt when we arrived in Israel and Steve's brother was plainly unwelcoming towards me. As the days wore on, however hard I tried, he could barely bring himself to acknowledge me. During a particularly tense meal, he asked Steve – in my presence – to tell his 'girlfriend' to pass the salt. When Steve responded angrily, his brother denied he had been rude. Accused by Steve of not liking me because I wasn't Jewish, he answered, 'I know a lot of Gentiles.'

Steve swore, and I moved from the dining table to the room we were sleeping in, trying to blank out the raised voices I could hear discussing me. The next morning we left for a few days break in Tiberius, on the western shore of the Sea of Galilee. We stayed in a hotel with a beautiful garden tended by nuns, and visited a kibbutz to the east. Feeling refreshed, we renewed our efforts to be helpful on our return to Jerusalem, volunteering to help with redecorating and babysitting. But the atmosphere got increasingly worse. During Seder, I made the mistake of asking questions about the rituals around Passover. I wanted to appear interested and engaged but my ignorance only served to emphasise the fact that I had no place there. I went to bed depressed, desperate for inclusion, knowing I would never find it there.

The visit was cut short and we escaped to Tel Aviv and then to the resort of Eilat before returning to London. When we went over to Steve's parents I was more sensitive to how they responded to me and began to notice ways in which the family revealed their disapproval. His father's withdrawn, vaguely irritated look as he opened the door; Steve laughingly telling me that in the kitchen his mother had suggested that I needed to find a 'nice Christian boy'.

I could not belong. I was an interloper, and consequently unacceptable.

Over thirty years have passed since Steve and I lived together but we have kept in touch. It is the winter of 2016 and he comes to my house, the house we shared all that time ago. The doorbell rings and at the front door stands a Jewish man in his late fifties. He has a white beard but the same youthful, mischievous eyes. And what do I seem to him: a tired woman in late middle age? My dress is shapeless, my hair is roughly scraped into a clip above my neck. I have made no effort to look nice or appealing. I don't want to impress or attract. I simply feel a sisterly fondness and the curiosity to unravel what happened in our past, what was shared and what was different, even difficult. I want to talk about identity, about belonging. About the things we seemed unable to discuss at that time.

The digital recorder is turned on. My first question sounds stilted, with its edge of earnestness and formality, as if I were a nervous and inexperienced journalist starting out on an assignment.

'I'm interested in your Jewish identity. Do you think there is something one can define as "Jewishness" and what does it mean to you? Has it changed over the years?'

Steve answers that his brother has a very different perspective on his religious identity than he does. 'I ended up with a Jewish family, but looking back on my life so far, I feel I was damaged very badly by my family because I felt I had a sense of freedom and independence which didn't necessarily contradict my love of being Jewish.'

'You mean they found that threatening?'

'Yes, they found that threatening. And they were ambivalent. For example, when you and I were having a relationship, my mother found it very hard to reject the idea of us being together because she loved you. But I think the rest of my family was ambivalent and I felt that very powerfully indeed. And it's one of my great regrets in my life that I didn't allow myself to have a guilt-free relationship with somebody who wasn't Jewish. And that happened again and again because after we broke up I had some relationships with other women who weren't Jewish. Until one day, via therapy and other things, the penny dropped: that I didn't have to feel guilty. Fortunately I began to grow up a bit and wean myself off that dependency on Jewish guilt. And that does exist, there is that guilty thing in Jewish families, if you're a guy you can't go out with a shiksa. And you were a shiksa!'

A memory flashes through my mind. It is about 1983 and we are in Blooms, a Jewish restaurant in east London. I think it was the only meal I ever ate with Steve's family outside their home. I kept unintentionally saying all the wrong things, like asking for butter with my bread. We finally reached the end of the meal when I asked for some milk with my coffee. Steve's father raised his eyes at the waiter in desperation.

'She's not Jewish,' he explained wearily, his shrug of despondent resignation saying it all.

As I froth the milk for our cappuccinos all these years later, I ask Steve, 'And you grew up did you, imbuing this information – shiksas being a no-go area – without it being necessarily said?'

'Yeah, yeah,' he answers taking the mug of coffee from me.

'Funnily enough,' I say thoughtfully as I sit back down, 'I can't remember it being a problem with us at the very beginning – it became an issue once we had been together for a while. But the difficulties we had at the beginning for me weren't about you being Jewish. Was that something going on in your head that you didn't share because you didn't want to bring it into the relationship?'

'No, no, Vanessa. Truthfully not.'

'I did feel the sense of difference between us – I don't know, I'm trying to get back into my younger brain – but maybe for me it was something to do with class. I had rejected the "poshness" of my family and, being half Italian, I was attracted to "the other".'

'Well, yes, me too, vice versa…'

'So it was more about that.'

'But that was what was successful about our relationship because…'

We then say in unison… 'We both felt like "the other"!'

Steve carries on, 'and we enjoyed that, I think for me that was what was wonderful, that you were from a different social milieu, culturally and in terms of class. All of that was exciting to me…'

'…and it wasn't as if it was a world you didn't understand because you were interested in art, in culture…'

'Yes we had a lot in common.'

'I remember you saying something at the beginning about being intimidated by me being an art historian!'

He laughs. 'You know, I've always been someone bad at controlling what comes out of my mouth! And it's a shame I said that because I wasn't intimidated really. I was deeply interested in that respect, in awe almost.' He pauses. 'I was intimidated every time I spoke to my brother about you.'

'I hadn't realised you spoke to him about me at all.'

'Yes, like when I told him we were coming to Israel.'

I am relieved Steve has mentioned it. I want to be honest, so I say, 'That trip was such a disaster for me, and you know the funny thing is, all I was thinking when we planned it was "how lovely, we're going on holiday to Israel!"'

Steve laughs again.

'...And I'd never been to Jerusalem and it seemed terribly exotic. I think for me I hadn't taken it all on board until there was clearly an issue with your brother that I wasn't Jewish.'

'You were in the eye of the storm!'

'Yes, for me it was just... "so you're Jewish, so what, I'm half Italian".'

'You were right, I don't think you need to readjust anything in the frame there.'

'That's why I found it so difficult. That holiday was really hard...'

'I know...'

'I initially interpreted your brother's coldness towards me as pure dislike. I told myself it must be because I'm inadequate, boring. I remember being so chirpy when I arrived, I even brought them a present, and he was so cold. I admit, I need a lot of validation, a lot of stoking before I feel OK with new people.'

'Don't we all?'

'So the fact that there was such a difference between you two siblings, the fact that you're so warm and he so cold, was hard to understand. I remember this kind of ice emanating out of your brother, I was being wrapped in ice and feeling really out in the cold. And being me, it triggered all my insecurities.'

'I think to an extent what you're saying is nothing to do with Judaism. These are issues that my brother has as a person, Judaism or not.'

'You mean he is quite a reserved person anyway?'

'Yes he is like my late father was; my mother was very gregarious like I am.'

Steve's mother was large and warm and welcoming. She wore tent-like dresses and treated Steve like a little boy. Steve reveals a bit later on in our conversation that even at his wedding she whispered in his ear, 'You'll always be my baby.' I liked her, even if I did discover once she had been round to my house when my mother was staying and Steve and I had both been out at work. My mother told me, 'She came to try and plead the case for you to break things off with Steve. She can't see how it can work.'

I ask Steve about Marta, his sister-in-law.

'To be honest I think she facilitated my brother's coolness and withdrawal. He has never been challenged by it. At the beginning I was very close to her. I was fifteen when Paul met her and I was very infatuated with her. She was beautiful, exotic, she was from Argentina, and yes, she was Jewish. They separated for a while then they came together again.'

I remember Marta as very attractive but distant. Perhaps she was just preoccupied by her small children then.

Steve continues. 'I think what happened on that trip we made to Israel was acutely hurtful to you and I feel very sorry about it. I also feel it damaged my relationship with you but it also opened something up inside me that made me realise "I don't want to be like this." But unfortunately it took me a while. I became very depressed from that time over a long period and found it hard to keep my relationships going. I don't think that had anything to do with my Judaism. My Judaism has become something very comfortable, something very positive in my life. If someone made a joke about my being Jewish, I would be able to accommodate it, as my kids would, because they are secure with what they are and how the world works.'

'So if someone should ask you about yourself, about your identity, would your Judaism be one of the first things that you would think?'

'Yes, yeah.'

'So who are you?' I ask it light-heartedly and we both laugh.

'Would you say "I'm a filmmaker who is Jewish," or would it be the other way round?'

'I would say I'm a fucked-up individual who is British Jewish, I'm a father, husband, filmmaker, friend. My religion is being Jewish and I love that, and I don't see any difference between the cultural side and the religious side. And I feel much more relaxed about my children marrying in or out and that's something I've really come a long way with. But most importantly I feel I've jumped back a generation. I'm more like my maternal grandfather. My dad didn't get it, he was very defensive about his "Jewishness", he was hidden, withdrawn. He loved it, he was proud of it but it wasn't a big public thing. Me, I'm much more like my grandfather who was British to the core. Even if he was probably born in some Russian *shtetl* – he didn't even know where he was born – he was very dapper, always wore a tie and he loved to watch the 3As athletics at White City, he loved putting money on a horse and yet he loved being Jewish as well, he was imbued with his Jewish roots and his Jewish culture and I aspire to that. And I'm thrilled that I was born into this country at a time when I didn't have to go through what a lot of Jewish people had to go through – Jewish and non-Jewish. I feel what a lot of immigrants feel, glad and proud, not in a pathetic way, it's like this world is my oyster, it belongs to me.'

'You don't feel threatened by the potential interfaith marriage of your children, that your faith will become diluted?'

'I thought I would, and at the beginning of my marriage I was probably a lot more concerned in that respect, even anxious, to the point of overreacting, for example, in sending my children to non-Jewish schools. I feel a lot differently about it now funnily enough. And I have been led to this by my children because my kids are secure in their Jewish identity which must be something we've done right. They will choose who they will end up with – gender, religion, all of those things are down to them. I don't get anxious when I think of these things, and that is different from my parents who did get anxious.'

'What do you think your grandparents would have said?'

'I think they would have been less angry and hostile than my brother was to you. I don't think they would have been more than puzzled, for them it was so much the norm that Jewish people married each other – it was just what happened. And Jewish kids didn't question it so much, it was much less of an issue in the immediate post-war years, whereas now, both my sister's boys have married non-Jewish women who have embraced Judaism and taken it on in a form that they can live with. They've done a reform conversion.'

Privately I wonder whether they felt pressured but instead I ask, 'How would you feel about one of your kids marrying a non-Jew?'

'I would try and love the person they loved. Funnily enough Rachel has a boyfriend at the moment who is Jewish; I wouldn't dare to mention it now. I'm working hard not to be biased in his favour because he's Jewish, but the point is he is a nice young man and that's why I'm happy he's my daughter's boyfriend.'

As he speaks I'm thinking about my own daughter Ellie. Her present boyfriend is Jewish. His parents include her in family gatherings and give her treats – gifts, theatre tickets. They are kind and generous and seem to like her, but I'm wondering how they really feel.

I bring myself back to the conversation in hand. 'After you and I split up did you reach a point where you thought, "I want to find a wife," as it were, "and she will be Jewish"?'

'Yes, I did. For you, does that contradict my saying I'm Mr Broadminded?'

'No, I think we are made up of contradictions, that's what we are in essence, what makes us human. It doesn't surprise me in any way.'

'But it kind of liberated me a bit – I had one foot in the old tradition and one in the new way of thinking. My kids are entirely new thinking. And in order to feel secure, I still needed to have that foot in tradition.'

'Yes, I see.'

'I got married in a synagogue in the traditional way and we spent a lot of time and energy proving to the authorities that we came from an orthodox background otherwise we would not have been allowed to have an orthodox wedding. And for Sofia's mother it was a source of some anguish because she didn't have any paperwork because she had come out of the Holocaust and yet the authorities...'

'You'd think they would understand!'

'They don't understand. We had to go to a great aunt in Budapest who managed to locate her grandparent's wedding certificate and if we hadn't found that we wouldn't have been able to get married in an orthodox synagogue.'

'I see your Jewish identity – interestingly, considering displacement and exile in the history of the Jews – tied up with being part of a community. About being rooted in a place.'

I have been thinking a great deal lately about 'belonging' and what that might mean and I tell Steve that his having an identity based on faith is something I quite envy. 'It is something I really lack and miss, especially as I get older. I have need of a spiritual dimension outside myself, rooted in community. But I don't feel it at all. I don't feel I have a church or a place. And that makes me feel very ungrounded and unearthed.'

'But you are a stable, rooted person.'

'I don't think I am at all! When my Rosa died I got some amazing support from friends but when the whole matter of the cremation, the memorial and the interment came up, I had no connection with it as a spiritual practice. I did it all because I needed to have some form of ritual around the death. I recognise that it would be wonderful and helpful to feel a comfort from within. You've spoken about going to the synagogue and your dialogue with God – whatever "God" means – and that is your personal dialogue, your conduit to something other than you. If you can identify yourself as a Christian or as a Jew you have a place in the world. I can't do that. My parents were atheists, I was never taken to church. There were no rituals. I felt bad when Rosa died that I was using Christianity by availing myself of a priest, a church, because I needed the ritual. When the vicar came to see us and said "now shall we pray?" both Andrew and I said "no thanks" and then I felt terribly guilty in case I had offended him, and sad, for I could get no comfort from that.'

'Look, I chose to get married in a synagogue and my determination to go through with the paperwork got it out of my system. As soon as I'd done all that my parents just slipped away, they got off my back, it no longer matters to me, it was like parents relaxed, I relaxed, everyone relaxed.'

'So I'm going to ask you a hypothetical question – one of your daughters comes home in a few years and says, "I'm pregnant by my non-Jewish boyfriend and I'm not getting married." You cool with that?'

'I hope so. I'm not going to start throwing plates around. I think I've changed. I can't feel worked up about it when you ask me the question now. The most important thing in my life is that my kids love me and that I love them and that they're OK in the world. That's the most important thing in my life and if she came home with that smile on her face… as long as we treat each other with respect and tact…' He laughs. '… and I admit I never used to be like that, I was a bull in a china shop and I was quite impervious to other people's feelings. I was troubled by your feelings about Jewish identity but I didn't know how to handle it, I didn't have the confidence in myself to handle it and that's a shame because we both suffered at the hands of the same people. You probably suffered more but I think I did as well and I'm glad we survived...'

'Well it's good to be able to talk about it all.'

We have been talking for over an hour. I know we have reached the end of that particular conversation. But there is still something bothering me, something unresolved.

'There's the whole issue that we never discussed... I don't know if we've got time.'

I'm tentative, hesitant, craving reassurance. I'm wondering about his parking ticket running out, about whether I should bring up the next subject that I have carried all these years.

Steve presses me to carry on.

I take a deep breath.

'About me getting pregnant.'

We have never referred to this since it happened, a month into our relationship, a long time ago. Should I continue?

'When you lose a child... if you're a woman... which you won't know about!' We both giggle nervously. 'The fact of pregnancy... the fact you know your child nine months before the father does, you feel it, even at the beginning. You feel it emotionally and physically because you feel different. I carry this guilt about the abortions I had, and that I took the decision to abort our child away from you. It was like, "I'm pregnant, I know what I have to do, I shall deal with it," with no real – and I want to apologise for that – with no real consideration of what you might have felt about it, and no processing of it. It was also tied up at the time with this political thing around "a woman's right to choose" which was so strong at university, which I now feel much more ambivalent about although I would never dream of telling a woman what she should or shouldn't do with her body. But it's not as straightforward as it seemed then. You always carry the scar of that. I did anyway.'

'On that level I was able to accept your decision.'

'You mean from a feminist standpoint?'

'Yes because I had come through Sussex at the same time with the same system of beliefs, and to this day I am glad about that. And I still believe that some of the political principles are fundamental but I agree with you there is some complexity... but that doesn't address one's feelings.'

'I don't know what I'm saying here, but it's something we have never talked about and I wonder if you'd ever thought about it or if you had ever revealed to anyone that this being had ever existed at all?'

He doesn't answer.

'Maybe it's different for men but I think of my children as Ellie and Rosa and then the little ones I haven't known... I feel that very strongly.'

Silence. I wonder what he is thinking. Have I gone too far? I feel my words have stumbled out without any control.

'Steve, I don't know what I'm saying or what I'm asking you.'

'You're not,' he says gently, 'you're telling me a lot actually.'

He pauses and laughs before repeating, 'you're telling me a lot!'

I say, 'And I know it was thirty-five odd years ago but I often think, you know, it would be this age or that...'

'I have thought about it a lot. And I have spoken to some people about it. And...'

Pause.

I continue. 'When I said that about your daughter of course, I wasn't making the connection...'

'No, I wasn't either...'

'But my God, what if we had gone together, me having never met your parents, and told them I was pregnant! It was right at the beginning, we'd only just got together...'

'Here's the thing,' Steve pauses. 'It's only been in the last three or four years that I have consciously been able to grieve for my – for our – lost child.'

'Oh, don't, you'll make me cry...'

We laugh again, despite my eyes brimming with tears.

'...Because grief has become very central in my life,' he says. 'I'll tell you actually when it really became apparent to me. In my own life I've faced the near loss of a child, which is not the same as losing a child, but when Sarah [his youngest daughter] was born critically ill and we were on a thread sometimes, I was reminded of the choices... and although your decision had been unilateral in that immediate sense, I knew we weren't ready to have a child together.'

'No, I know.'

'And it was the first time we'd slept together! But I will tell you now...'

Pause.

'...I have a lot of regret and... I was very deeply in love with you.'

My tears are brimming again.

He continues. 'I was. So I think that also affected my relationship with you, and what happened with my brother. I was angry with my brother for being mean to you, and I was angry with him for having his own children. He would say things and I would think, "How dare you say that to someone I would have been able to have a child with?" And it was a double thing, because it wasn't as if I did want to have a child with you because, as we've said, we weren't ready. But in another hypothetical situation we may have had a child, we may have had a life together, and I don't need my brother to stop me from that.'

'Yeah, yeah.'

'And I think now I'm able to feel that comfortably without being embarrassed or be embarrassing. We both have our lives and our families now. I don't think my parents ever knew, or my sister. But I have shared it with my wife and she is very sympathetic.'

'Yeah...'

'So I'll keep that bit complicated if you don't mind, I'll keep that bit difficult... I'm never going to think "oh she was the wrong person and wasn't Jewish and thank God we didn't have a child together". I'm never going to feel that.'

'That's the thing really, because I think I treated it at the time as.... But...' I can't find the right words.

'I don't know,' he interrupts. 'You took me in, you took me on board with all my baggage, I had nothing and you took me into your home, and I was a bit of a freeloader and I was a bit unfaithful and yet you're definitely one of the great loves of my life!' He laughs self-consciously.

'Ah, well you were to me too.'

'And I'm quite comfortable with that. And yes, I put you through some bad times and so on...'

'Well, I wasn't brilliant either...'

'No! So it's good that we can sit at the table now, thirty-odd years later! Go on, put it in your story. Write what you want to write. Because you know, I think it's a bit of a red herring, the issue of Judaism and Jewish identity. I think what we are talking about now, in the past five minutes, are the really fundamental things. And neither of us is grasping how that relates to religion. I cling to my nice Jewish community and you can't feel at home with Christianity but actually what those faiths say they are really about, is love. All that love is, is the messy everyday stuff...'

I want to ask him about his unfaithfulness. As we are here unpicking things, I'm not going to let that go.

'The whole aspect of unfaithfulness... I found that a very threatening thing, because in the act of your unfaithfulness I felt,

"I mean nothing". And because I've had problems with feeling I am "something", I found that very hard…'

'Yes, yes…'

'…that we couldn't work things through in some way. That you had to sabotage everything.'

'Good word.'

'But you know, I admit, I was complicit. I was looking at an old diary and it seems that every other day I had a headache or a migraine, and I'm thinking, my God I must have been a drag to live with!'

'Oh yeah! But it was the chicken or the egg – who was giving who the headache! Well, there was a lot of tension… But it was brilliant as well, I think we had a good time!' He smiles.

'We did. But really what bugged me was finding out about your unfaithful moment the night before you left Paris to come to live with me in London…'

Steve looks blank.

'You know, with the black dancer at your goodbye party.'

He laughs. 'Oh yes!'

Is he pretending not to remember?

'I had actually sensed something when you arrived. You know, I was so excited about you coming to live with me, it had been wonderful in Paris…'

'Oh yes…'

'Well, there you were, leaving Paris to come and live with me in London, and I was excited. It had been so romantic in Paris. And then you arrived in London looking sheepish, and I remember at the time just knowing something had happened, something had changed.'

'Oh yes, that was right at the beginning…'

'What upset me so much when I discovered this years later, revealed by your friend David, was that I thought we were so in love…'

'But… if I can interject a moment… I never referred back to this in my mind. Not because I was ashamed of it in any way but because it wasn't a significant moment for me.'

'That's interesting…'

'It was just one of those moments, I wanted to try something different.'

'Yes I understand that. But the point is, even though it may not have meant anything to you, it did to me.'

I decide not the mention the other time, the deep hurt when he slept with a girl I had thought of as my friend, after we had been living together for a year or so.

'You know, I wasn't aware enough of that in you, and I think I still repeat that. It doesn't stop just because I've been in a stable marriage for twenty-five years and we have three children. I'm not perceptive enough.'

'So what you need to do…'

'I steamroller…'

'OK, Steve, so this is my present to your wife… You need to be sensitive to the fact that even if sometimes the thing that doesn't mean anything to you, for whatever reason – a reason that may not be your fault, or not instigated by you – there are triggers that can bring out suffering and insecurity in your partner.'

'These are interesting collisions. Saboteur is a good word. It's not even malicious, evil sabotage.'

'You were like a puppy spaniel, adorable and trusting, who would just leap into anybody's car…'

'That recklessness was my downfall for a long time.'

'Yes but it was also your charm.'

'Yes but it stops being charming after a while. It becomes a bore, for both yourself and the people around you. And you have to start defining yourself in a more boundaried way. You have to.'

* * *

We speak more about relationships with partners, with children, with parents, with oneself. Of dissonance and connection, of expectations unrealised. I realise that as a young woman I was always searching for an ideal, and he couldn't live up to that, as I couldn't to him. Maybe he is right, that the question of faith is a red herring. But whatever the motivation for this conversation, it is good – and Steve agrees – that we can sit at the table now, thirty-five years later, uncovering the stones and dismantling our defences. We can finally accept our human fallibility and the differences we could not accept then.

Mary

I have been thinking about Mary, who died in 2012, two months after her ninety-fifth birthday. Only a few years ago that seemed so old, and now my own mother has overtaken that point in her life. I wouldn't presume to call Mary a 'friend', but I knew her for many years and always enjoyed talking with her. A few days after hearing that she was seriously ill, I went over to her house. As I walked I planned our conversation. I would get her to talk about aspects of her past, about her memories of life in Kent sixty years ago; of the job she had had at the Tollgate – a delicatessen that no longer exists in Tenterden, a local town; of the tearoom she ran in the oast house at the castle in the 1970s and early 80s; of her famously delicious scones which I had loved eating when I used to stay at Sissinghurst with my cousins. I had heard her stories before but only the happy ones. I learnt the sad ones after her death.

Her daughter Linda opened the door and warned me that Mary had not slept for forty-eight hours. She was on large doses of morphine. I stood in the doorway of her bedroom, taking a moment to observe her before she had a chance to notice me. I was anticipating frailty, but even so her appearance was shocking. It reminded me of my Italian grandparents Nonna and Nonno and Uncle Nigel when they were approaching death – thin and shrunken, with that grey and sallow complexion, as if the blood was already cold in their veins. For a second I felt dread in the knowledge that in the not far distant future my own mother would look like this.

Poor Mary, she looks like a corpse already, I thought, before managing to compose myself as I entered the room.

'Hello Mary!' I said cheerfully. Her eyes were empty as she looked up at me.

'It's Vanessa,' I continued, a bit too loudly, taking one mottled, bony hand in mine.

Her eyes seemed to flicker with recognition.

'Hello dear.'

'You look nice and comfortable,' I said, and she did, propped up against a mound of pillows. Her body made hardly any form under the starched sheets and the pretty, flowery bedspread.

'And what a lovely view!'

Linda had placed her mother's bed in front of the window so that she could look out over the garden and the Weald of Kent beyond.

'Yes, it is lovely,' Mary whispered.

I scanned the room, struggling to find something innocuous to say. On the bedside table were framed black-and-white family photographs. A young woman with pearls around her neck. A man in spectacles, another in uniform. Her husband? One of her sons when young perhaps?

'Who is this?' I asked, pointing to the man in glasses, hoping this might trigger a memory or thought and provide us with something to talk about.

Mary was staring at me but did not answer.

'Hmm?' is all she said.

'This man,' I asked, as I walked around to the table, picking up the photograph. I put it in her hands.

She looked confused. 'Hmm?'

I was feeling self-conscious.

Is it too early to say goodbye? Maybe she's tired. Can I go now?

'I was just asking, who is this handsome man?'

The photograph fell into her lap because she didn't seem to have the strength to hold the silver frame. It lay forlornly on the bedspread, one of her hands slightly covering the man's face.

Then Mary spoke. She fixed her gaze to the right of me, as if someone was standing there.

'Oh, look at your lovely daughter.'

Her words chilled me to the core.

'Would you like a drink dear?' Mary asked the invisible person.

'I… she…' I began.

'Has anyone offered her a drink?' she asked, looking around at the empty room.

My heart was beating very fast.

She's dead Mary. My lovely daughter is dead.

Mary was my closest neighbour and had lived near Sissinghurst most of her life. She survived not only the death of her husband Stanley but also that of her two younger siblings and two of her four children. Like so many of the generation that lived through world war, she met the hardships life threw at her with resilience and courage. When times were tough she made the best of the situation and opened her mind to new possibilities. Everything she did, she did with a will.

It was her father, Captain Oswald Beale, who had farmed the land and through a family connection had introduced my grandmother Vita to the 'castle' at Sissinghurst in 1930. In 1921 Oswald's wealthy father had bought Bettenham Farm near Sissinghurst for his son to run and his growing family to live in. But agriculture hit hard times in the late 1920s and the farm lost a lot of money. Mary would recall the heartbreak for her father and the farm workers when the whole of the hop harvest was sent back from London because there was a glut of the crop and little demand. The hop pockets were slit open and the contents were spread on the fields: a year of investment, labour and income, all gone to waste in an afternoon.

Vita and Oswald came to an agreement that she would buy Bettenham and lease it back to him so that he might pay off his debts. He would then run both Bettenham and Sissinghurst farms together. He made a success of this but money remained tight. His daughter Mary was bright and would have liked to train as a teacher but any available funds went towards her brother John to help advance his education and medical training. Mary stayed behind to help her mother with the house and look after Jean, her sickly younger sister.

At the beginning of the war a writer called Ian Davison was living in a medieval hall house called Branden, near Sissinghurst. His book *Where Smugglers Walked*, published in 1935, is the story of an old haunted house in the Weald of Kent which had sheltered weavers, smugglers and devotees of black magic, and is based on Branden. It was here in 1939 that Ian Davison entertained Commonwealth officers and here that one weekend Mary was introduced to Stanley Stearns, a Canadian pilot with RAF Coastal Command. They married in 1940.

Jean, Mary's younger sister, smiles out of the wedding photographs, a pretty girl who was only twenty-two when she died from the kidney failure that had dogged her life since the age of three.

At the end of 1941 Stanley went back to Canada to train pilots, and Mary followed him with their firstborn James, who had arrived earlier that year. It was at the height of the U-boat crisis and the journey took two weeks, as ships crawled across the Atlantic in convoys that were under constant threat of attack. It must have been terrifying – never going faster than the slowest boat, never knowing which ship might be successfully targeted by German submarines.

Once in Canada their second son Michael arrived. They lived in straitened circumstances: lugging the pram up flights of stairs to grim flats in Montreal and Quebec, hemmed in by drying nappies and unfriendly neighbours. Despite the support of her sister-in-law, Mary felt far from her family and the Kent countryside.

By the end of the war Mary and Stanley had gone back to Sissinghurst with their little boys. The farm business had become arduous for Oswald and it made sense for Stanley, who had managed a farm in Ontario before the war, to return to England and join forces with his father-in-law. Another son, Richard, was born to them in 1946, then a girl, Linda, in 1949.

The family lived in the house at Bettenham until my uncle Nigel put it up for sale on the death of my grandparents in the 1960s – he had to raise money for the endowment required by the National Trust in order to accept Sissinghurst Castle and the surrounding estate. He always felt guilty about the forced sale, however, and twenty years later he offered a pair of estate cottages he had inherited to Mary and her son-in-law at a favourable price. They bought and converted them. Mary lived in one, and her daughter Linda still lives with her husband Brian in the other. These are the only houses that can be found between mine – Horserace – and the castle estate.

Over the years I would regularly see Mary when out walking my dog. She was always smartly dressed, or as her generation would say, 'well turned out'. Her coiffured hair had a purple tinge and her lipstick was carefully applied. After she had died I remarked on her elegance and Linda laughed affectionately, remembering her mother, bedridden but groomed to the end, insistent on maintaining standards: 'Darling you will tell me if I've got too much lipstick on…'

When Mary and I met we would stop to enquire after each other's health and maybe comment on the weather, and occasionally reminisce about how Sissinghurst used to be before the tourists came. She would remind me of the times when cattle grazed in what is now the car park, or how East Enders would camp for the annual hop-picking. Her nostalgia was sometimes tinged with sadness but it was never sentimental. Linda told me that when a few years ago my cousin Adam was hoping to galvanise the National Trust into returning Sissinghurst to a mixed, traditional working farm, her mother had responded to his bucolic idyll with resignation: 'You can't go back, you know...'

One time Mary invited me to stay a while, and as we sat in her garden enjoying the summer sun and drinking lemonade, she told me about being introduced to my Italian mother in 1955. It had been hop-picking time and Luisa, engaged to my father and a guest at the castle, had asked Mary all about the farm and the history of hop-picking in Kent. Luisa had grown up on a farm in Tuscany owned by her uncle, and as a child had been well aware of the importance and hope attached to the success of the annual olive harvest. The two women had warmed to each other. Luisa found her easy to talk to and, doubtless, less intimidating than her future in-laws. Mary, in turn, always spoke fondly of Luisa.

Mary was a practising Christian and her faith was important to her. Captain Oswald Beale was a respected member of the local congregation when he died in 1957 and Mary and her brother John donated, in his memory, a pair of tall, beautifully carved, wooden candlesticks for the altar at St Dunstans, the imposing medieval church at the heart of Cranbrook, our local town. A dish runs around the rim of each candle and every Easter Mary would fill these with primroses. She needed quite a few to do this, and if Easter came early she would worry that there would not be enough available. So in early spring she would ask if she could take some primroses from our garden and the surrounding woods. I can see her still, cheeks flushed and smiling with the flowers in her hands, thanking us, relieved to have achieved the task she set herself every year.

She suffered so much loss in her life. Her sister Jean had died when Mary herself was still a young woman. Her husband died in front of her in 1967 of a heart attack. He was in his early fifties. Her third son Richard had suffered with emphysema and died in middle age, the year before his brother James collapsed and died coming back from holiday with his wife in South Africa.

Linda, her youngest child, recounts how she, James and Michael climbed the stairs to their mother's bedroom that morning in 2006 to inform her of Richard's death. Fifteen months later Linda was – in her words – 'trundling up those same stairs with just Michael, to tell her about James. I thought we should both be there, you see... but the look on her face when we told her... she couldn't take it in.'

James and Linda were the ones I knew, for they lived near me. I would see James virtually every week, his tall figure loping around the Sissinghurst estate, running his farm shop or propping up the public bar at the local pub. Every time I went into the Three Chimneys he was there, drinking his pint and chatting in his lugubrious tone with local farmers dressed in tweeds and flat caps. His mournful eyes and voice were in contrast to his ready smile – he never failed to stop and ask how we were doing. He had run the farm for a while with his father, but financial problems led him to diversify into other small businesses – the Sissinghurst tearoom, the farm shop, a bed and breakfast he ran with his wife Pat in the Victorian farmhouse next to the castle. And then in February 2007 he and Pat had gone on the fatal holiday to South Africa to celebrate their 40th wedding anniversary. He died as he was doing up his seat belt in the aeroplane, waiting to come home.

James's death hit Mary hard. Coming at a time when she was still grieving her other son, it must have been particularly difficult. 'She didn't talk about it,' Linda says, 'But she went into herself for a while. That generation didn't break down.'

On 3 September 2008 Mary had come to my daughter Rosa's memorial service in Cranbrook Church. 'You know it's Mary's ninety-first birthday?' her son-in-law Brian told me as we stood outside the church following the service, and added, 'she insisted on coming.'

I smiled sadly at Mary as she took both my cold hands in hers – the day was unseasonably chilly and I had chosen a thin cardigan that had belonged to Rosa to wear over a summer dress. She said something kind about words not being adequate. It felt strange, a ninety-one-year-old coming to the funeral of a nineteen-year-old, a reversal of more than just numbers. I had not been fully aware then of what had happened to her sister or of her other losses, apart from James.

Shortly before her own death Mary became worried that she hadn't said goodbye to James properly. Much later Linda told me how, throughout the time her mother was ill, she called out for Stanley and for James. 'I want to be with my husband and my oldest son,' she would cry. Both had died so suddenly while in apparent good health, Stanley in front of her, on an ordinary day while mowing the lawn. Mary's son Richard and her sister Jean had suffered longstanding illnesses, and however painful, perhaps this made those two deaths slightly easier to come to terms with.

But that morning in her house, propped in that bed, what or whom had she seen in that room? Rosa? The ghosts of all my other children who failed to be born?

'Has anyone offered her a drink?' Mary repeated.

It's the morphine talking, of course it is.

'No, no, she doesn't need a drink...' I stammered.

'What about your other daughter?' She was looking to my left. 'She is lovely too isn't she?'

'No... yes... no, thank you none of us need a drink.' I said, a bit too curtly. Suddenly I craved a double whisky.

Got to think of something else to say. Change the subject.

'I'm going to Florence in a couple of days. To see Luisa.' My voice was artificial and high-pitched.

'Luisa?'

'Yes, my mother Luisa.'

Mary lifted her head and peered at me intently.

'Does she have a husband?'

'Well yes, but he died, you know, Ben...'

'Oh my dear, I'm so sorry.'

Concern and sorrow filled her voice, as if he had died yesterday.

'No, it's fine, it was a while ago.' I smiled awkwardly.

Think of something else to say.

Mary was looking at a space by the window and before I could speak again, she said in her wobbly voice from another age, 'Look, your son is here too.'

I followed her eyes to the side of the window, as if I really did have a son standing there, or should have had. And then I slowly bent down towards her, picked up her discarded photograph and placed it carefully back on the bedside table.

'I really should go now.'

Mary's expression had not changed. 'Your husband must have been so pleased to have a son,' she smiled, eyes looking at the empty space.

'Yes.' I stood for a few seconds absorbing this, before pulling myself together.

'Well it's good to see you. You get some rest now.'

'Yes dear, goodbye.' She sounded weary as she closed her eyes.

'Is there anything I can get you?'

Silence.

'Goodbye Mary.'

I left the room. Brian and Linda were in their kitchen. I opened my mouth to say something reassuring but a sob escaped instead of all the sensible and comforting things I had meant to express. Linda reached her arm out towards me and as we embraced she began to cry too. 'I'm fine until someone is nice to me,' she said. I squeezed her shoulders, brushing the tears from my cheeks as we parted.

'Linda,' I wanted to say, 'I'm crying for the grief that lies ahead for your family. I'm crying because Mary looks so loved and well cared for here, and this has touched me.' But my tears are also for all those ghosts standing around in the room next door; ghosts of people who existed and for the souls of those who never did, seen only by Mary as they wait for her to accompany them to another place.

It is summer again, close to another anniversary of Rosa's death. As time goes on, these significant dates that punctuate my calendar with pain seem to come around so much more quickly. That's what older people say isn't it, how time speeds up as the body slows down? And here I am, an older if not yet elderly person, saying these things.

But I'm not quite ready to welcome the narrowing of everything into dark corners of familiarity. That's why I regularly attempt to shake my life up. I do new things, I move around, I travel, I lose touch with an old friend but make a new one, all in order to try something or somewhere or someone new, to avoid getting trapped in routine. And when the sad thoughts do inevitably follow behind, I can even find some solace, for it connects me to grief and to Rosa, the object of that grief. Will that fade, and will the lessening of that intensity bring with it its own sadness? Or should I hope for the kindness of memory loss and decrepitude to remove some of the rawness I still carry?

My only fear is that I shall end my days demented but still reliving my past in a fog of sadness and longing, pointing to a faded photograph and boring some distracted nurse about my beautiful nineteen-year-old daughter who died. 'Yes, Mrs Davidson, you've told me that already,' she will say, followed by a muttered, 'yes, actually several times.' Or worse, no comment at all, perhaps just an irritated sigh accompanied by a roll of the eyes.

Would it be better to die young before there are too many sad events to remember? Before the potential indignities of old age become humiliating? It's become an obsession of mine, working out ages from dates marked on tombstones and in obituaries, wondering at the randomness of the cards we are dealt, searching for clues. Maybe it would be easier to be like Mary, and trust that God will decide who, why and when it is time to leave, and go, looking forward to being reunited with those who have left before us.

3

FRAILTY

Vanessa

She was hiding in the bathroom of a cheap hotel and the man was waiting in the next room. He was there, just on the other side of the thin door she was leaning against, and it didn't seem to her that he was in any hurry to leave.

The bathroom was small and lined with tiles. Large white tiles everywhere, floor to ceiling. A plastic stool under the window had a couple of towels stacked on top that she removed before sitting down. 'God I'm tired,' she whispered to herself as she wiped her hands over her face. The weariness was overwhelming, and she longed to climb between those cotton sheets on the bed that beckoned so tantalisingly next door.

'You OK?' said the man's voice, on the other side.

'Yes, yes,' she answered, more to herself than to him, as she tried to pull herself together.

I could have a shower. But then I will have to come out of the bathroom in a towel. Unless I put my dirty clothes back on.

'You have shower?' The man had a thick, heavy accent. It was friendly, but louder this time.

'Yes, shower...'

The stool was so light that it toppled over as she stood up and pushed it away, but she left it lying where it fell. Slowly she turned on the rusting tap of a tiny basin, placed too low for someone of her height. She unwrapped the round bar of soap that had been left on the side and, as she washed her hands, looked in the mirror. Lank hair, bags under the eyes, a pasty, yellow tinge to her skin from the fluorescent strip. She was still wearing the T-shirt and jeans she had put on twenty-four hours previously, before taking the tube to Heathrow.

I wish he would leave now.

It was August 1979. In London she had left behind a heatwave and a tearful Ed, the gay American friend she had met at university who was heading back to New York. Her plane was scheduled for the evening, and she was feeling emotionally drained before the long flight to Athens had even begun. After landing she was to take a bus to the port of Piraeus, followed by a ferry to Monemvasia where her friend Jenny was waiting. The flight was slightly delayed and the bus from airport to port took longer than expected. She arrived in Piraeus at 4 a.m.

There was hardly anyone around but she stopped to ask a handful of official-looking men in turn, 'Boat? Monemvasia?' They indicated spots further and further from the place where the bus had let her off, worrying her that she would never find the right ferry. She continued walking, with the weight of her rucksack getting heavier, until she finally saw a notice: MONEMVASIA.

To the right of the sign was a booth with a little glass window that looked like a ticket office, but the window was drawn closed with something written in Greek propped up against it from the inside. As she was peering in and around the booth, another man walked past.

'Ferry at 9 a.m.,' he said.

'Oh, but I...' She had hoped there would be an earlier one.

But the man walked on and didn't turn as she shouted after him, 'please, excuse me!' to ask for more information.

She looked at her watch. Around four and a half hours to go.

Thank God she had eaten on the flight, and she had some water left over. Despite being the middle of the night, it was warm and balmy, with a gentle breeze. There was a bench running against a wall near the ticket booth. She would curl up on that, lean her head on the rucksack and try and catch some sleep.

As she settled in to rest, a couple of young boys appeared.

'He-llo! He-llo!' they chanted.

She smiled at them guardedly, then placed her head on the rucksack and closed her eyes.

'Hell-o! He-llo!'

If I ignore them they'll get bored and go away.

'He-llo! He-llo!'

It sounded like a chorus now, and she opened her eyes. More boys had joined up, about six of them now, ranging in age from about eight to thirteen.

What are they doing out at this time? Why aren't they at home in bed?

'I need sleep,' she said, sitting up, closing her eyes and leaning her cheek into the prayer gesture she had made with her hands.

'English! English!' they chanted, and then there were more boys, circling around her, grinning.

'I need... sleep,' she said again, more slowly this time, and laid her head back on the rucksack.

'You have cigarette?' one of the older boys asked.

'No I haven't. Please go away,' she pleaded, unwilling to get them out of the rucksack pocket.

'I think cigarette here.' The boy began prodding the shape made by the cigarette packet.

'OK,' she sighed, resigned to getting the packet out and distributing the cigarettes. The boys swarmed around her like mosquitoes. One particularly nippy one dived through the outstretched hands and tried to grab the rucksack but she managed to push his hand away.

'No!' she said as firmly as she could. 'Now please... please go home.'

They would not leave her alone. In desperation she looked around for somewhere else she might move to, for some uniformed person to walk by and shoo them away, but she was pretty sure that if she did get up and look for another place, they would follow her. The best thing was to try and shut them out.

That plan didn't work. The boys soon became bored with prodding the rucksack and began trying to pull it from under her head. 'GO AWAY!' she shouted, and they ran off, laughing, only to return half an hour later, just as she was dozing off, to resume their torture.

It was light by the time they finally gave up their game. Her nerves were frayed from lack of sleep. She was worrying about how to let Jenny know that the ferry was leaving later than they had thought. She had the address of where Jenny was staying – a house belonging to a friend's parents – but there was no telephone there. They had planned a post-university break but Jenny had gone in advance for a few days with her sister, and they had agreed to meet her off the ferry early that morning. What would Jenny think when she went to the harbour and she wasn't there?

She looked at her watch. 6.30 a.m.

She must have dozed off because she was woken by the sound of voices. There were signs of activity as men – they all seemed to be men – bustled up gangways, undoing metal chains and generally looking occupied.

She yawned and stretched. Her neck was stiff and she had a cramp in her side. She tested the stiffness by moving her head from side to side, then looked at her watch. 8.40 a.m. The ferry would be here soon. She must get a ticket.

Looking around, she saw that the glass window was still closed. There seemed to be no other passengers waiting to board, in fact there was no ferry to be seen that looked as if it might be ready to leave, nor any arriving. There was just a group of middle-aged Greek men chatting and a few stray cats. She walked closer.

'Monemvasia?'

'Ferry?' She pointed at the sea. 'To Maw-nem-vaa-see-ah?' She enunciated every syllable, hoping this might make her clearer.

A man came forward – short, swarthy, balding – with an enormous belly, wearing a stained T-shirt and badly fitting trousers.

'No ferry. Ferry in two days,' he said in a strong accent, lifting up his thumb and forefinger.

'In two days?' she repeated, anxiously. 'But the one now, at nine o'clock?' She pointed at her watch. 'The man said...'

'No, you come Thursday morning.'

'But I can't,' panic rising, 'my friends are waiting, I have to get ferry right now...'

He shrugged, and went back to join the group of men.

Her hands were sweating now. She took a deep breath, then shakily pulled one of her remaining cigarettes out of the packet and lit it. Only four left, those bloody boys. She inhaled deeply. Taxi. I shall get a taxi. She remembered her father always telling her that should she find herself in difficulties abroad, she simply had to hail a taxi and ask for the British Embassy. Or was it the consulate? She imagined a tanned, smiling consul dressed in beige linen, coming out of an office and saying in clipped tones, 'Don't you worry Miss...' And then what would he do? Anyway it was probably too early for the embassy to be open. Well, she could wait outside. The thing to do right now was to find a taxi.

She dropped her hardly smoked cigarette and extinguished it with her foot, grinding it into the ground, then walked purposefully up to the group of men. What were they? Fishermen? Dockers? Ship workers? They didn't seem very busy. Maybe one of them might be able to tell her where she could get a taxi.

'Excuse me,' she interrupted, smiling tentatively, 'Taxi?'

They all stopped talking and stared at her. Then one man broke from the group and came reluctantly forward, beckoning for her to follow him and get into a car – marked Taxi, she was pleased to see – parked a few feet away.

She settled into the back seat, rucksack on her lap and said with some relief, 'British Embassy please.'

The driver half turned towards her, expressionless.

'Embassy?' she repeated.

Nothing.

'British consulate?' she said this loudly with no effect.

She asked again, this time enunciating the words very clearly. 'I would… like… to… go…' she took her passport out of her pocket and pointed at the image of the Lion and the Unicorn on its cover. 'British Embassy?'

The man was shaking his head.

OK, let's try a different tactic.

'Hotel?'

The man nodded and waited for her to say more.

Oh no, he wants the name of a specific hotel.

'You know… hotel? Or hostel? Youth hostel?'

Blank. He waited a few seconds, then he made a sort of waving, 'you wait here' gesture and got out of his car. She craned her neck and could see him returning to his group of mates, who listened as he pointed towards her in the taxi. Hopefully he was asking for suggestions regarding a hotel?

One of the other men separated from the group and tapped the window of the car. He was the big-bellied one who had originally told there was no ferry until Thursday.

'Come, come.'

'You take me to hotel?' The pigeon English was infectious.

'Yes, I take you to hotel.'

She got out of the taxi and followed the man to another car. This one was not marked Taxi and she hesitated slightly. The man had opened the boot and was pointing at her rucksack.

'British Embassy?' She tried again.

'No, embassy closed. You go later. I take you to hotel first.'

He sounded impatient. She felt uneasy.

'Please,' he said more gently, reaching for the rucksack. 'You no worry, my cousin have nice hotel. By sea.'

A hotel by the sea sounded tempting. And what was the alternative, stuck in the port with no ferry? She would ask the receptionist at the hotel to contact Jenny and then she could sleep. She was exhausted. And the man? She studied his face: weathered, middle-aged, adorned with full, dark moustache. He probably had a house full of kids. Judging by the circumference of his belly, his wife fed him a lot of moussaka.

She offered him the rucksack and he threw it in the boot. Would it seem rude to sit in the back of the car? Yes, she must sit in the front she thought, opening the passenger door. The car smelt of stale cigarettes. There were various objects dangling from the car mirror – religious beads and paraphernalia and a sepia photograph in a small frame of a rather fierce-looking woman in her forties. His wife or perhaps his mother. All reassuring.

As the man turned on the ignition he looked at her and smiled for the first time. He definitely looked trustworthy.

'Thank you for your help,' she said, sounding as friendly as possible. 'I am very grateful.'

'Very good. I take you to hotel now, then goodbye.'

'Yes,' she answered, returning his smile, 'and then goodbye.'

What a kind man. She trusted him unquestioningly. As she rested her head on the window she daydreamed of freshly laundered sheets and sleep.

They drove along a coastal road, holiday apartments and resort hotels on one side, the blue sea on the other. Gradually the beaches gave way to rocky coves and after a few minutes the man turned left and stopped the car in front of a building that looked as if it had only recently been completed.

'We here. I come in to say hello to my cousin.'

She followed him up the curved stone path and into a dark reception area. She saw with some relief that it looked basic, because she did not have much money. Cheap furniture in imitation of mahogany, a 'vase' holding dusty plastic flowers on a sideboard, a strong smell of bleach emanating from recently washed floors. She could see a small dining room to the left, and shiny stone stairs leading up to the rooms ahead.

The receptionist was reading a newspaper spread out in front of him. He looked up reluctantly as they walked in. Was this the cousin? The greeting between the men seemed less than familial, in fact the receptionist did not reveal a flicker of recognition. The man went up to the desk and began talking, loudly.

She held back. He was gesticulating and pointing at her and she couldn't understand a word but she smiled timidly, hoping they would hurry up so that she could get into her room. The receptionist was scowling. What was the man saying? Why was this taking so long? Perhaps he was simply explaining her situation, the problem of the ferry not running for two days or some such thing. Whatever it was, the man at reception didn't soften. After listening to the man's speech he shrugged, glanced at her, turned and took one of the room keys from the hooks behind him, passing it to the man and then looking back down at his paper.

'Does he want my passport?' she asked, used to the custom in Italy, where some form of identity was required before any room was allocated.

'Later. I show you room now.'

'I suppose it's a family business,' she said out loud as she followed the man up the stairs, but he didn't answer. She was too tired to care about the hostile, almost disdainful look the receptionist had given her before turning away.

The room, like the reception, was basic, small and anonymous, but at least it was clean. She threw the rucksack on a chair and turned to the man to thank him, but he had walked across to draw the nylon curtains closed as if it was night-time and he was staying there too.

'You go to bed,' he said.

'Yes,' she answered, 'I must sleep.'

There was a pause and he didn't move.

'Well thank you for your help. How much taxi?'

'No taxi, you are my friend.'

She giggled, nervously.

'Yes, your friend. Thank you.' She wished he would just go now.

'I tired too. I sit here,' he pulled up a wooden chair. 'I sit and you sleep.' He was still holding the key.

'I… I have to have shower first.'

'You have shower, I sit.'

She frowned, hesitated, and opened the door to the bathroom, then clicked the lock shut. She leant against the door. It did not occur to her to be firm, to say 'thank you, but I need to be on my own now, please go'. She was indebted, she couldn't do that, had he not rescued her? If it had not been for him she would still be trapped at Piraeus. At least she had a room now. He was just tired, like her, he needed a rest before going back to his wife or whatever he had planned to do that morning.

She sat on the bathroom stool, stood up, looked in the mirror. She tried to blot out running thoughts of being trapped, taken hostage. She felt so grubby. She wanted to get between those sheets feeling clean, not dirty.

Maybe I shall have that shower after all.

She turned the shower on and took her clothes off, leaving them in a pile where they fell. The water kept running cold and after a minute or so she stopped waiting for it to warm up. It was so hot outside and quite a relief to feel the water cooling and cleansing her body. But it was too cold to enjoy staying in there for long. She came out with hair and body dripping wet. The towels were a bit small for her but she took two of them and managed to cover herself by holding them in place with both hands.

There was a knock on the bathroom door.

'I need bathroom,' the man was saying.

She unlocked and then opened the door wide and walked out of the room. He looked her up and down as he passed, brushing against her shoulder.

I must get some sleep.

She grabbed a big T-shirt out of the top of her rucksack and managed to put it on quickly before leaping into the bed. Her hair was wet and uncombed but the room was hot, it would dry.

I shall pretend to be asleep.

She closed her eyes as he came out of the bathroom.

He was standing by the bed. 'Are you married?' he said.

She paused, then still with her eyes closed she answered, 'I'm getting married. When I go back to England, I am getting married.' She wore no ring, but hopefully he hadn't noticed that.

There was silence and she opened her eyes. He looked tired and old, fatherly almost. She didn't feel threatened. Something made her continue. 'Yes, I am getting married in a church in the country. I have a beautiful white dress and my sister is being a bridesmaid. My father will walk me up the aisle…'

None of this was true. She did not have a sister and her father had died the year before. She was infatuated with a boy she had slept with once but could hardly call him her boyfriend, let alone fiancé. She didn't even believe in the institution of marriage.

The man was standing, listening. 'Why your boyfriend not come? He leave you alone?'

'Oh no, that's it, that's why I had to get the ferry.' She transposed Jenny into Mr Right. 'He is waiting for me in Monemvasia, he will be wondering where I am.'

That's a point, how do I tell Jenny I'm here? I must let her know.

The man squinted, as if he did not believe her.

'He is staying in the house of a friend's parents. I need to tell him I am here.'

'You send him telegram.'

'Yes, a telegram, good idea.'

'He young man?'

'My fiancé?'

The man nodded.

'He is young. Very handsome, he...' Here she tried to think of a suitable occupation for him. 'He...'

'He should not leave you alone,' interrupted the man.

This wasn't fun. She wanted to sleep.

'I must sleep now...'

'I tired too,' said the man. 'I have sleep then I go.'

'But...'

I wish he'd just leave.

'No drive when tired. Bad luck.'

He sat on the bed and was taking off his shoes and socks. Now he was pulling his trousers down.

Fair enough, he needs to rest too. Maybe he was working all night. Then he will go.

He had climbed into the bed next to her.

She turned on to her front and buried her face into the pillow.

'You need massage, I give you massage.'

'No, thank you,' she mumbled politely, but he began kneading her shoulders anyway. After an initial shudder, it felt strangely good. Her neck was stiff and her shoulders so tense, and his hands were strong. He pulled her T-shirt up and began massaging her back, with firm sweeps across her aching body. It was unsettling, this mixture of repulsion and relief that his touch engendered. She didn't want to encourage him, but at best it was as though she was being treated by a physiotherapist familiar with knots of muscle tension. She lay very still and silent because she didn't want to give him the impression that she was enjoying any part of it. Any pleasure was underpinned by unease and anxiety.

'Now my turn,' he said. 'You massage me.'

Her heart sank. 'No, I'm sorry, I must sleep.' The thought of touching him made her feel nauseous.

He shook her shoulder. 'I gave you car ride. You must massage now.'

'No,' she said sulkily, as she shrugged his hand off her back and turned on to her left side to lie facing away from him, curling into a foetal position. She pulled her T-shirt down at the front but her back was still exposed, the material bunched up by her shoulders.

I'm so tired. Please go away.

He was fumbling around with his clothes. She could sense him behind her, sweaty, old, impatient, as he pulled off his underwear. He smelt of the port they had just left. A pungent aroma of fish and tar and dampness was seeping into the white sheets, destroying the scent of fresh laundry. Some part of her knew she should be angry, she should shout at him to leave, but she was ashamed, she was indebted, and a little bit frightened. He was rubbing himself against her back, masturbating now and she was frozen, every limb and muscle tensed, waiting and longing for it to be over. She tried to take her mind to another place, to a few days ahead, when she would be safe with Jenny on a beach or a cafe in the sun somewhere, laughing about the experience. She knew she would embellish the story to make it funny. It didn't feel funny right now.

She thought of the boy she believed she was in love with, of his fair hair and the smoothness of his youthful body, so different from this dark, panting, hairy, fat man. The boy was Saint Sebastian, he was pure and ideal and beautiful, her protector, martyring himself for her. She tried to remember as many famous representations of the saint as she could – by Mantegna (three of those), and the Perugino, and the Botticelli, and who painted the one in the National Gallery? And the man was grunting and she turned her mind to other paintings she loved, and she rose out of the dirt she felt trapped within and then it worked; she was no longer there in that bed, in that moment, she had left her curled up body behind and was far away walking along a beach, laughing with friends, and now she was in a bucolic English landscape; and then she was floating above the bed and she saw the girl, her right arm across her face, her wet hair across the pillow, but she didn't want to go back to her, not yet. So she returned to the countryside and there was a field full of cows and one of them let out a big sound and she realised that the man in the bed had grunted loudly and the two sounds had become one.

She was back in her body. She felt something sticky on her lower back. She didn't move. She heard him get up and go to the bathroom again. The sound of water running. She kept her eyes closed as she heard him shuffling, putting on his clothes. And then she sensed him standing by the bed. She was immobile, willing him to leave.

More shuffling, then a sound as if he were putting a key on a table, then the door opening, closing. But she kept those eyes shut for some time before daring to blink, to look around, tentatively as if he might still be lurking somewhere, knowing he could not be. She wanted to get up, to lock the door, to have another shower. She must go downstairs to send that telegram to Jenny. She couldn't move. She was drifting into sleep.

Many hours later she woke, still in the same foetal position, feeling hungry. Slowly she got up, and went into the bathroom. She stood once again under the cold shower, this time for much longer, as if waiting to be purged of the memory, of the shame. Finally she dried herself and dressed in shorts and a clean T-shirt before leaving the room and going downstairs.

There was a different receptionist there, a young woman.

'I would like to send a telegram please. To Monemvasia. Here is the address,' she said as she passed the scribbled note across the desk. The woman took it and smiled. 'That will not be a problem. I hope you will enjoy your stay.' She looked Greek, but her English seemed fluent.

'Thank you. Can I order some food?'

'Yes, supper will be served in the restaurant in half an hour.'

She walked out of the hotel into the soft, early evening light and crossed the road to the stony beach. Hardly anyone was around, just a few families and tourists collecting their things at the end of the day. She walked until she reached a rocky barrier preventing her from going further, but she noticed a flat surface within the rock and climbed on to it. The protruding stone against her back precluded any real comfort but the stone seat felt smooth and warm under her thighs.

She sat, looking out at to sea at the setting sun. Tomorrow would be different. Tonight she would ask the woman at reception how to get to the Acropolis, she would make good use of her free day in Athens before returning to the port and catching the ferry to Monemvasia the day after.

That night she could not sleep. It was the heat perhaps, or because she had slept in the afternoon. She kept trying to think of the things she planned to see the following day, filling her mind with images of ancient Greek art and architecture, of temples and statues, majestic and noble, ideals of beauty to replace and elevate her from the seedy visions that were taking hold, traces of which left a stain that lingered.

Em & Jean

When I was a schoolgirl I once asked Ben why he always put 'Church of England' as the answer to 'Religion' on any form he had to fill in. He was giving permission for a school trip or a passport application or something similar I had brought him to sign off on my behalf. I was standing by his long oak desk, watching and waiting for him to finish.

'It's simpler this way,' he said, not looking up.

'But we never go to church or anything, so you are sort of lying.'

'We don't have to go to church to be Church of England, it's just the closest religion to what we are.'

'Do you believe in God then?'

'Well, not exactly…' he seemed distracted as he carried on going through the form.

'So if you don't believe in God does that mean he doesn't exist?'

Ben stopped writing for a moment and looked at me over the top of his spectacles. 'Philosophers have been asking themselves that question for hundreds of years,' he smiled.

I changed tack. 'What about mad people then? What if you're mad and you think you're Napoleon, but you're not really are you?'

Ben abandoned the form for a moment and reached for another cigarette. 'What do you mean?'

'Well if someone says they believe in God, it's like saying they are Napoleon, it doesn't mean he really exists, but he does for them.'

'You are funny, Vaness.' He chuckled as he picked up the matches. 'I suppose if you're mad and you think you're Napoleon, there is no harm in that. Unless of course you start acting like Napoleon.'

I frowned. 'But that doesn't answer my question.'

I know it isn't simply about irrational behaviour, of being so outside an acceptable definition of normality that sequestration is the only alternative. Madness is something terrifying and uncontrollable and there is no kindness, no compassion, in the treatment of it. Not in my experience anyway, not at that time, not in that prison of suffering. That space, both inside and outside my head, was so brutal and frightening and I fluctuate between extreme gratitude for having left it behind, and terror that I will have need to return there.

And what about the ones who remained, who were unable to escape? I often wonder what happened to Em and Jean, how long they were trapped inside that terrible institution, what lives they might have lived since. If they managed to get back into the outside world did they survive there? I hope so. But for all I know, they could both be dead.

Our bond was intense during the course of seven days and I have never forgotten them. This occasionally happens when people with nothing in common are thrown together. I have experienced this in more enjoyable times, on a course for example, or when travelling solo: the sharing of an intense experience with strangers when finding oneself removed from anything or anyone familiar. We turn to those who are there out of a basic need for connection and we can briefly feel more attached to them than to those we have known a long time. Usually the experience is forgotten as soon as we are returned to familiar territory. But the memory of Em and Jean has remained with me.

The road that led me there began nine months earlier with a bout of the flu. I was a student, a 'mature' one this time, studying for an

MA in London. Twenty years after graduating, I was back to writing essays and checking footnotes, requesting discounts at exhibitions, explaining to the younger students that I had to rush to the station after lectures to catch the train back to Kent to make supper for my children or oversee homework, so no, I couldn't join them in the bar later.

The winter was a bleak one and despite being engaged with my studies, I was beginning to get tired and run down. Finally, after a morning spent at the university struggling with a bad cold and unable to contribute to a seminar, I took an earlier train home and went to bed. I stayed there for a week, feverishly off my food, coughing continuously, unable to concentrate on the reading material stacked up by my bed.

And then I did the sneeze. It was an incredible sneeze. A long intake of breath had travelled slowly up through my lungs and throat into my nose, then paused for a few seconds before erupting into a climactic cacophony of sound. As I surrendered to the expulsion of air I felt something odd, a dislodging in my lower back – like a 'clunk' of hidden matter, falling. To what, I wondered?

But I seemed all right. I recovered from the flu and went back to the MA. My weeks divided into four days as a student, one day doing intern work – part of the MA course – at the National Portrait Gallery in London. Most of my time at the gallery I spent carrying files from the basement, several flights of stairs down, up to the offices. My task then was to order the contents of the files and note what was included, before returning them to the dusty passages underground and collect more.

One day a gallery employee found me sitting on the back stairs with my head on my knees.

'My back – it's terrible, it's agony, I can't move...'

It had been getting increasingly painful, to the extent that pills no longer helped to numb the pain. I was fed up with a body that always seemed to get in the way of me pursuing what I wanted it to do. I'd find something interesting to occupy my mind and there it was, undermining me, sabotaging my plans, dampening down my energy and stamina. Migraines had afflicted me for years, now my stupid back. At least the academic year and the work placement were coming to an end. I would be able to stay in the country and enjoy the summer with my family. I left my final afternoon at the gallery smiling, my face obscured by a vast bouquet of flowers – a leaving present from the gallery staff.

But I could barely walk. Standing and sitting were just about possible but the bits in between were more problematic. Over the next two months, I went to osteopaths, chiropractors and physiotherapists, but no one was able to alleviate the pain more than temporarily.

'Can't you go and have an operation or something?' Andrew finally muttered impatiently after weeks of me grumbling and stumbling around the house. I couldn't turn over in the bed and in the morning it would take me an age to lever myself on to my feet. Even brushing my teeth was excruciating as I couldn't lean forward towards the basin.

'I shall refer you to have an MRI scan of your back,' my GP was saying. 'But it may take a few months to get an appointment.'

I couldn't wait months! What was I supposed to do? Then I remembered Charlie, a friend who had undergone a back operation a year or so before. He had spoken effusively of Mr Scott, the orthopaedic surgeon at the Chelsea and Westminster Hospital who had sorted him out.

The following day found me on the way to the fracture clinic of that hospital. Hours of waiting, and then no bed immediately available, but Mr Scott admitted me as an emergency once he realised I wasn't even able to get on to the bed for him to examine me. Within twenty-four hours I had had the MRI scan and my operation was booked.

'You have a slipped or bulging disc,' the surgeon told me. 'This problem can usually right itself, but in your case the disc is jammed against the spinal chord. We shall perform a partial discectomy tomorrow morning. There is one thing I have to warn you about. There is the possibility of nerve damage.'

'What does that mean exactly?' I asked in alarm.

'You might lose some feeling in your leg, or there could be more serious paralysis. But this is unlikely.'

The night before the operation I could not sleep. I was certain that I would be in the small percentage of patients suffering serious and permanent paralysis. How would I manage without being able to walk? How would I cope with the children? How would I drive them to school? By morning light I was sure that in a few months I would be in a wheelchair without the use of my legs, relying on Andrew to do everything for me. It was bad enough having to ask him to put socks on my feet...

The operation was a long one. It had all been explained to me but I didn't take in any of the information. I was wheeled off, shivering in an extreme state of dread, worried about the paralysis, convinced that the anaesthetic wouldn't work properly and I would wake mid-operation but that nobody would notice. I kept muttering to myself 'pull yourself together' as I shook uncontrollably – looking back, I can see I was in some state of shock, processing the information I had been given. The nurse and the porter had to wrap me with blankets to calm the shaking as they wheeled me into theatre.

'Count down from ten,' the anaesthetist said as he put the syringe in my vein but I was still awake as I reached number two and I heard the nurse laughing, 'you're difficult to knock out!' before darkness descended.

I woke up groggily, hooked into a morphine drip. My friend Minky was at my side.

'I can't feel my legs!' I shouted.

Concern crossed Minky's face.

'My legs! I can't feel them!' I shouted again.

Minky got up to find a doctor. And then a nurse was next to me, trying to calm me, advising me to administer more morphine from the contraption attached to my arm.

'Please get a doctor,' I pleaded. I didn't trust the nurse, she looked too young and inexperienced, what would she know about paralysis? But she kept telling me to calm down, the operation had gone well, there was nothing to worry about...

'I need the doctor!'

Everything I had ever been taught about not making a fuss evaporated into a desperate need for reassurance. I was convinced I was going to have to live without the use of my legs. I couldn't bear it. I would never be the same again.

Finally the doctor on duty arrived. He too was young, and looked tired and hung-over. He sighed as he sat by my bed but tried to reassure me.

'The operation was a long one, but it has been successful. Mr Scott will be round to see you later.' He tested my reflexes and pressed on different parts of my right leg. I couldn't feel a thing.

'You may have some numbness in your right foot but that should fade with time. You will not be able to get up for a couple of weeks and you will be shaky on your feet at first but I promise you, your reflexes are fine.'

And with that he fiddled with my morphine drip and I felt a medication-induced peace seep through me.

The doctor was right. Three weeks later I was back home. And yes, I had numbness in my right foot (I have it to this day) and I was not allowed to drive for six weeks, but I was euphoric that everything had gone to plan. I could walk – hesitantly – but I could walk, and I would enjoy a peaceful summer, recovering, catching up on my studies.

* * *

It was in October that I began feeling odd. At first it didn't seem that strange. When the children went back to school in September a familiar flatness had taken hold but I attributed it to the prospect of winter and the stress of the back pain and the operation I had gone through. I was supposed to be working on research for my MA thesis but I was losing the momentum. This was normal I told myself, I often went through periods of unexplainable torpor; the sluggish lack of energy, the longing each morning for the day to end. This could last for weeks sometimes, and then would lift. But this time it wasn't lifting and things needed to get done.

My GP was sympathetic as he wrote out the prescription for an antidepressant that he said might help improve my mood. I left the surgery feeling positive. Prozac. The magic pill. It would take the flatness away and would enable me to function again.

Two weeks later I was feeling much worse. The anxiety was tangible – I couldn't sit still, my legs were constantly shaking, I was always jittering up and down. My heart beat furiously. I felt weird and disconnected. Driving along, I would suddenly wonder where on earth I was heading. One day I found myself parked at the side of the road, bewildered and lost, not knowing how to find my way home.

I returned to the GP as arranged. 'I feel terrible,' was all I could say, not meeting his eyes.

'You need to give the pills time to work,' he said. 'I'd like to see you again in a couple of weeks.'

I began having violent fantasies about killing myself. In the past when I felt life was not worth living, I would fantasise about going to bed with pills and floating off into oblivion. This time it was different. I was thinking about knives, about stabbing, about jumping off cliffs, or driving the car at speed and crashing it against a wall. Most of all I thought of ropes and loops and hanging, I could imagine myself swinging, my feet pointing downwards, my neck slumped to the side. I didn't want to fade away peacefully. I wanted to destroy myself using excessive, brutal force.

I was unravelling, disconnected from everything that rooted me: work, family, friends. The only moments of peace were granted when I curled up in a foetal position on the floor by the tumble drier. I would put it on even though I hardly ever used it to dry clothes, and I found that the noise and vibration would calm me down, as if I was *in utero*, listening to a mother's heartbeat.

Back in the waiting room at the busy surgery I wondered how I was going to manage until the time my name was called. I could not sit comfortably. I squirmed about. I leapt up to get a magazine, sat down again, then up to get a different magazine. And then, oh no, I realised that on the chair next to mine was a local woman, friend of my uncle Nigel.

'Hello Vanessa, how are you?'

I looked at her as if she were a strange creature in a zoo or an aquarium, behind reinforced glass.

'Um, hello, yes thank you, very well.'

Ten walls of glass between us.

'How are the children?'

'The children?' For a second I forgot that I had any.

'Oh yes the children, yes, um, the children...'

Got to be normal. I pinched my arm to ground myself.

'Are you all right Vanessa?'

Can't do this. I was sweating profusely. I had to leave. I would come back another day. I looked at this elderly lady with her bewildered expression and suddenly the whole waiting room was full of faces, staring at me, expecting something from me, and they would be there when I came next time. I would never be able to return because this would carry on happening on a loop and then how would I ever get to see the doctor?

'I'm sorry, I have got to go to the loo...'

I stumbled towards the bathroom, the door flying open because I had pushed it too hard in my desperate need to escape. I slammed it shut. Door locked. Thank God, I was finally alone. I was gripping the basin, breathing heavily. As I looked up I saw a crazy woman in the mirror, like *Kate's Madness*, the painting by Henry Fuseli inspired by William Cowper's poem *The Task*. Hair awry, wild staring eyes. I looked away. Where could I hide? I spotted a space between the lavatory and the wall. I squeezed myself into that space, arms hugging my knees and waited, relieved to sense the wall on one side, the lavatory on the other, containing me. I just had to wait and this would pass, and the lady in the waiting room would be gone, and all those other faces would disappear and I would be OK. I tried to slow my breath to calm my agitated heart.

There was someone knocking at the door, calling my name. The receptionist had watched me go into the bathroom and was saying that the doctor was ready to see me. I had to leave my haven.

A young man was sitting with the doctor in the consulting room. 'Hope you don't mind a medical student sitting in on your appointment?' I shook my head.

He asked how everything was going 'I… don't… feel… right…' I spluttered as I sat on the chair offered me. I was pulling the sleeves of my jumper and scratching one hand with the other and jigging my legs and tugging at a strand of hair and then I was telling them that I couldn't manage at all.

'Do you have suicidal thoughts?' the doctor was asking gently and the visions of stabbing and hanging flashed through my mind and I looked at my lap as if ashamed and mumbled 'yes' very quietly and when I looked up again the doctor was saying that maybe it would be for the best if I went to hospital for a while, 'where they can help you', and the medical student was nodding and the doctor was making phone calls and asking me whether Andrew could drive me there.

We drove in silence. It was as if I had already arrived somewhere else. Finally I was calm, imagining a bed all for me in a white room, clean cotton sheets. Peace.

But when we got there it looked more like a prison than a haven. A group of prefabricated huts stood on the edge of the Victorian hospital (now all demolished). Andrew was asked to wait outside as I was 'interviewed' in one of these huts by a man and a woman, whom I presume were the psychiatrists. The woman was dark and heavily made up, with long red manicured nails. I couldn't take my eyes off the nails. They asked me a lot of questions that seemed irrelevant – what was my level of education, had my husband put pressure on me to get admitted?

I just want to feel better. Please make me better.

'You're all fucking like rabbits!' a man with an enormous head was shouting as I was shown into the main Nissen hut. It was a dismal space that contained a dining and sitting area on the right, accommodation on the left. Andrew had gone, looking upset. I felt blank, an object, a thing to be dealt with. The woman with red nails led me through a heavy security door and along the long corridor with beds to the right that made up the men's sleeping quarters. Another heavy door past a few more beds. The woman stopped and pointed to a cubicle: a single bed, a small table, a narrow window overlooking a brick wall. Thin curtains on either side offered some privacy from the other beds. I noticed a shadowy figure of a woman lying on the bed opposite. The space next to mine was closed off by the curtain.

'The nurse will come and take some details,' the woman was saying and walked off.

I sat on the hard bed and looked at the bag I had brought with me, stuffed with a few clothes and toiletries. I hoped I wouldn't be staying long. I slowly began unpacking my things.

Suddenly there was a noise like a long zip unfastening, as the curtain to my left was pulled briskly across to reveal the neighbouring bed. A pale young woman with goth-dyed hair and black clothes to match was standing just inches away from me.

'Who the hell are you?' she sneered. I felt I was back at boarding school, facing an older, anorexic version of the bully who used to taunt me in our dormitory.

No escape.

'Hello, I'm Vanessa…' I mumbled.

'Oh-er, very posh, "hello, I'm Vanessa,"' she mimicked in a sing-song tone. 'Well I hope you don't bloody well snore Vanessa, 'cos I haven't got any fucking ear plugs…' She picked up the packet of Prozac I had placed on the bedside table. 'You won't be able to keep these here you know, they'll take 'em away,' she said as she played with the packet in her hands. 'You got any diazepam?'

I could hear footsteps. Before I had time to answer, a middle-aged nurse had appeared. 'Leave Vanessa alone, Em,' she said as she pulled the curtain closed again.

Em had been right. The Prozac were taken away along with the headache pills, tweezers and nail scissors the nurse found in my washbag. I had to fill in forms and I was given information about the unit: meal times, location of bathroom and smoking room, how to swipe the security lock to get into the women's ward.

While the nurse was talking I became aware of a distant whimpering sound, like a trapped animal.

'What's that noise?' I asked, interrupting.

'Oh, don't worry about that, it's just Jean. Tea is in half an hour, don't be late,' she said as she stomped off back down the corridor.

I waited a moment, expecting Em to reappear behind the curtain, but she seemed to have settled to reading a magazine. The whimpering continued and I got up and peered into the gloomy corridor. Across the way there was a large shape on another bed, and it was from here that the whimpering sound was coming from.

'Are you all right?' I said into the darkness. The whimpering got louder. 'I want to go home,' a voice said.

I walked over to the bed. There was a large woman aged about forty-five whose short hair looked as if it had been badly cropped with nail scissors. She was cross-eyed, with a pinched nose and blotchy skin. The palm of her hands and several fingers were wrapped in flesh-coloured bandages, the sort my mother wore on her swollen ankles during the summer.

'Are your hands painful?' I asked.

'Arthritis,' she answered very softly. Her voice was like a child's.

'Are you in pain?' I asked again. 'Can't you ask the nurse for something?'

She shook her head.

'You think the nurses here give a shit?' Em had appeared, looking angry. 'You could drop dead here and they'd only care about you making a mess.' She came over to Jean's bed and in my anxious state I froze, thinking she was about to lash out at me or Jean and then what would I do? Where had the nurse gone?

But she didn't. She came over and gently stroked Jean's head. 'Poor baby,' she said tenderly as Jean leaned into her bony shoulder. I watched them, this strange pair that seemed like a damaged mother and daughter. I was a witness to their moment of intimacy.

It was suppertime. They called it supper but it was still only about 5 p.m. I hadn't eaten all day so I was hungry but when I saw the food my heart sank. Again I felt as if I were back at school. I sat poking at gristly stew trying to find a vegetable but nothing resembling one was in evidence. The man with the big head was still shouting about rabbits. Another man was ranting about being Eric Clapton. Two women were staring at me suspiciously.

I was part of this. Here was my tribe now that I had entered this society of the insane. I am one of the mad, I thought, and I shall never get out. Worse than 'Mad Kate', I am like those agitated women in old photographs of Bedlam, to be pitied and laughed at and despised. I have become somebody else, who am I? I want to hold my children. I want to be held by Andrew. How desperately I crave the familiarity of home.

Then I dropped the fork I had been holding and started crying. Noiselessly at first, then increasing loudly. I felt a hand on my arm, a hand covered in beige bandages. 'Don't worry,' the voice said, 'you'll get used to it here.'

'I don't want to get used to it!' I sobbed and couldn't stop, and suddenly there was the nurse moving Jean out of the way, and the woman with the red nails, and they were offering me a glass of water and pills, or was it an injection? – and once I'd gulped them down or been injected they were dragging me back through the corridor of men's beds and then into the women's section and then my own bed and then I fell asleep.

It was very dark and silent when I woke. I had no idea of the time and couldn't find my watch. I needed to pee. As I got up I felt myself swaying, but staggered across the corridor and managed to open the door of the bathroom. But the dizziness overtook me and I felt myself fall.

I was on cold linoleum. I don't know how long I was lying there but I couldn't move. I could hear a troubling sound, like a Middle-Eastern wail for a dead child. And then loud footsteps running and the nurse saying 'that's all right Jean, go to bed…' and the nurse was trying to get me into a wheelchair and pushing my head and shoulders back as I kept slumping forward. She wheeled me to my bed and she wanted me to stay sitting in the wheelchair but I still felt dizzy and was desperate to lie down. In the end I had to swipe her away as she tried to restrain me. I threw myself face down on the mattress as she protested angrily.

A male doctor was called. The nurse complained about my uncooperative behaviour as he took my blood pressure.

'When did you last eat something?' he asked. I shrugged. I had no idea.

'I think it's a blood sugar thing. Get some hot chocolate and toast,' he ordered the nurse.

That hot chocolate and toast were the most delicious combination of things I had ever tasted. I felt the warmth suffuse my body and my energy return. But as soon as the doctor left I was moved to a single room to be 'observed' for the night. Despite my protestations that I was 'fine now', my jailer stood in the doorway, arms folded, watching me as I fell into fitful sleep. Whenever I woke the nurse was still there.

This little drama got me some attention from the other patients, and they were friendlier. 'Hear you spent the night in the isolation room,' the deluded Eric Clapton said at breakfast. 'What you here for?' asked someone else. 'Depression I think,' I answered, not being quite sure.

But I was still nervous of Em, who kept darting me hostile sidelong glances. As soon as breakfast and the queue for medication had been dealt with, I returned to my cubicle and pulled the curtain around my bed. I closed my eyes and tried breathing into the agitation held in my chest.

'Hey posh girl!' the curtain was pulled open and there was Em again, standing by my bed. 'Put my stud back in.'

She knelt down and her face was right by mine, aggressive and confrontational. She was offering me something, and her other hand was pointing at her nostril, which was red and swollen.

'I don't think it's a good idea...'

'Oh, you "don't think it's a good idea" do you?'

'No, your nose looks infected, you should get that seen to.'

I realised I sounded sanctimonious rather than caring.

She laughed, more a cackle than a laugh, and prodded me with her hand. 'Put the fucking stud in.'

I did. I took the tiny object from her hand and rammed it into the angry swelling. She whelped.

'I'm sorry, but you said...'

'No, cool, thanks...' She looked at me and smiled. 'You're a princess, you.' Her whole face lit up.

Jean was whimpering again. Em and I looked at each other and walked across to her bed.

'You all right darling?' Em said as she sat on Jean's bed.

The three of us developed a friendship that became deeper as the days wore on. I was touched by Em's solicitude for Jean. 'She's got no one,' she said when Jean was out of earshot. 'Bastard husband dumped her here. Treated her like shit, beat her up. Son died from drugs. I hear her crying about that.'

I would hear her too, at different times of day. She didn't move away from her bed much other than at mealtimes, and would lie still looking blankly ahead, holding herself very still as if waiting patiently for something or someone that never came. Em sometimes curled up beside her, her thinness just fitting into the tiny space left available. And occasionally I would join them too, perched at the bottom of the bed, three damaged figures finding solace in each other's presence.

Time dragged on. Apart from the meals there was no timetable or structure to the days. If I wasn't in my 'dormitory' I sat in the fug of the smoking room, just for the distraction of listening and observing. I hardly spoke. There were several fantasists. 'Eric Clapton' would talk about his gigs. Stories were told about successes and adventures experienced in the outside world. Maybe some were true, even. Or not, it didn't matter. Nothing mattered because nobody cared who you were or why you were there or what you believed in or what you had done. There was a kind of liberation in being or saying anything you wanted. You could say 'I'm a kangaroo', or 'I'm an addict', or 'I'm the Virgin Mary', or 'I want to die'. Nothing, at least not by the other patients, was judged or responded to with shock or fear or ridicule. And with that came freedom and a release of sorts. Anything could be believed or disbelieved at whim. A friend arrived to visit with a toy doll with wings and told me she had brought my guardian angel. That toy offered me more comfort than any drug, and I clung to her for days, truly believing that she was there to protect me.

It was only when Andrew or the couple of friends who came to visit saw the place, that I viewed it through their eyes: grim, institutional, unfamiliar, threatening. We, the inmates, took the occasional dramas – the uncontained moments of hysteria and shouting, the man constantly ranting about rabbits – as everyday happenings. This was our normality. Only the sane found it frightening.

The strange thing was that there was no therapy. No one seemed interested in trying to understand what had made us what we had become. We were simply fed bad food and managed with medication. There were half-hearted offerings of activities nobody took part in: the 'art room' was usually closed because there was no call for it or no staff available to supervise. The sports facilities were in a different part of the hospital and no one was able to take us there. We were not allowed to leave the Nissen hut, though once we were led around the grounds of the hospital, a strange group of odd-looking stragglers with nowhere to go.

There was the twice-daily queue at the medicine kiosk, when a grumpy nurse would pass across a little pile of pills and water, but any human interaction and care was left to the intense friendships made between patients. It reminded me of a crazy version of boarding school, not only for the bad food and beds and boredom, but from the way we had resigned ourselves to our misery and loss of independence, and our understanding that it was necessary and advisable to comply with the basic rules: take what you are given, expect nothing, departure forbidden. Abandon all hope.

I had spent only four or five nights there when I decided I had to leave. I gathered the little energy I had to focus on what I needed to do.

The first thing was to take charge of my medication. I had just enough sanity left to know that the Prozac was not helping. In fact it was making my anxiety worse. So I found a part of my mouth to hide the pills that were handed to me morning and evening. If you used your tongue to push them high enough against the gum above the back teeth you could even open your mouth when required and give the illusion that there was nothing in there. This could be followed by a trip to the bathroom where the pills were removed, wrapped in paper and flushed away.

I also knew I had to appear as sane and cooperative as possible in order to be considered for 'release'. This was more problematic as I felt neither sane nor cooperative. But I asked about using the art room to show I was interested in life beyond myself. I made a thin Giacometti-like head I was quite pleased with until a woman said, 'who is that?' and then I didn't like it anymore. 'It isn't anyone,' I snapped back.

I got myself up for the meals I didn't want to eat. I was courteous to the nurses. I brushed hair and teeth to show I was able to care for myself, though I had no interest in what I looked like. I was taking control.

Em and Jean on the other hand seemed resigned to staying in that place forever. I tried to talk to them about this, and to encourage them to envisage the world outside. I was a prisoner encouraging others to escape, to enlist help. But I soon got the message that they did not have much to return home to, whereas I had. When I asked Jean how long ago she had been admitted, she looked at me as if she had no idea how to answer.

I was more careful with my questions to Em because she could easily become aggressive. 'What's it to you?' she might say, both in response to questions to herself or to Jean, whom she wanted to protect from any possible distress. 'Leave her alone! Why are you so nosey?' But the next minute she could overwhelm me with friendliness and wit and we might even manage a three-way conversation, Jean, Em and me, and end up giggling like schoolgirls over the man shouting about rabbits or other insanities.

Seven days had passed and it was time for my weekly 'assessment'. This took the form of the two psychiatrists inviting Andrew, my next of kin, and myself into a room to discuss my 'progress'. I had decided that morning that this was my chance. 'You have to help me get out of here,' I had managed to tell Andrew when he had visited a few days before.

'Be normal,' I repeated to myself as the nurse came to fetch me and I was invited into the room. Although I didn't quite know what 'normal' was any more. I felt strange despite stopping the pills. Andrew was already sitting there looking concerned. He knew I was desperate to get out. And there was the nurse saying something about me being cooperative despite the lack of cooperation on my first night, and the doctors looking at notes, and Andrew making a case for my being transferred to a private psychiatric hospital nearby.

The doctors were asking questions. I didn't understand what they were asking. The room was closing in. I was sweating. Andrew was looking worried.

I have to get out. I'm not well. I need to lie down. Got to get out.

'I have to lie down!' It came out as a yell rather than a statement.

* * *

All these people are staring at me as I stumble up. They are telling me to calm down and stay, but I'm pushing my way out of the room and rushing to my little bed and throwing myself down on it and sobbing, not knowing why. And then Andrew is by my side, saying it's OK, you can get transferred. I've got you out of here.

He helps me pack my things. I have been given a letter to hand to the next people. Andrew is waiting with the car outside. I have one more thing to do.

Jean is lying on her bed as usual. Em is sitting on the edge, glaring at me. 'I'm leaving,' I say. 'I just wanted to say goodbye.'

Jean looks at me with panic in her eyes. 'You can't go!' she cries. 'You can't leave me!'

'But Jean I, I, I'm sorry, I have to go.' Stammering, I look for reassurance at Em, who darts me an accusatory look.

'Well, fuck off then posh girl…'

I'm in a car. I feel strange. Then I'm sitting in my own room in the private hospital. I even have my own en suite bathroom. 'Very posh,' Em would say. The food is better and they bring it to me on trays so I don't have to see anyone else. I'm not good with other people, they make me nervous, the doctors have understood that. When I leave the room to have a cigarette – I started smoking again in the last place – I bump into the woman from the room next to mine who tells me she is an alcoholic and that the bloke with the staring eyes who prowls along the corridors is a rapist. I get anxious when I realise I am unable to lock my door. At night I don't sleep thinking he is going to come in to get me, and I'm jumpy when the nurse on night duty opens the door to check on me. No, I'm not sleeping, but there are more pills to deal with that.

There is a doctor – McMillan, McTaggart, McDonald or something – coming in and talking to me with a Scottish accent. I confess to him that I have stopped taking the Prozac but I feel very anxious about the rapist and I can't sleep and I keep crying. He prescribes something else that empties my head. There's nothing in it at all. Not a thought, not a feeling, no pain, no joy. My brain is like a whitewashed wall. I want to hang a painting on it, something to look at, but nothing is there.

I stay a second week at the hospital, but it is expensive and we have no health insurance. I worry about that. I miss my children. I feel their absence like an ache in my chest. Andrew has told them with my agreement that I have returned to hospital to make my back better. I don't want them to know I'm lost.

I want to go home. I need to go home. That is where I will find myself again.

Kate's Madness by Henry Fuseli

Adam

I AM SEEING MY DAUGHTER FOR THE FIRST TIME IN SEVEN and a half years, hearing her voice, watching her move, recognising items of clothing long forgotten. She does not know I am looking at her – I, her neurotically vigilant, anxious mother – and it pains me to see how free and unfettered she is. I want to interfere, to say 'stop, be careful, calm down, watch out', but the beauty of the thing is that she is finally liberated from my control.

She first appears on ice. Oh no, I think, we were advised not to let her skate, for she had epilepsy and she might fall, and to drop convulsing on to the hardness of ice would be bad and dangerous. Rosa's friends are gliding around the rink while she wobbles near the enclosed edge, holding her boyfriend's hand, making jokes about being 'Bambi on ice'. And then suddenly she is managing to stay up on her own. She shouts enthusiastically. 'Let's skate, let's skate! Let's show everyone how wonderful we are!'

That's my girl, going for it.

Another film. She is on a rollercoaster at a fun fair. Oh no, we were told she should avoid amusement parks – the loud noise and strobe lights, the jolting, the increased adrenaline. But there she is, screaming with excitement, her beret flying off to gales of laughter...

Now she is in a house, apparently one belonging to her friend Charlotte's mother. This is the last film I'm shown. Two couples have gone to the house for a weekend while the mother is away. Rosa is pretending to be a TV presenter, grinning at the camera that follows her behind. 'OK! Hi guys, let me take you through, look how big this fucking kitchen is…'

I am strangely shocked by hearing the swear word come out of her mouth. She looks and sounds drunk and slightly hysterical. She is running upstairs. The camera follows. 'This is Charlotte and Owen's love room…' She sounds breathless. 'Look at this beautiful, beautiful room, my God that's amazing… now come on, downstairs… off we go again, here we go… and here's the living area. Look and… the beautiful balcony, balcony…' She runs around, leaping on top of the furniture, striking poses. She makes a joke about being 'so excited, I'm going to have an epilepsy seizure'.

She is too thin. She is being outrageous. I want her to stop.

'Calm down, Rosa, take it easy.'

As I watch her I am braced for the disaster I know is going to happen. She is spiralling towards it and I can't do anything to prevent it. It is as if the only outcome is for her to die young, as if death is stationed at her side like in those representations of 'Death and the Maiden', a bony phantom waiting for the moment to seize a beautiful young woman.

As I write 'seize' I am struck by the echo of the word 'seizure', the physical manifestation of the condition that took her life.

'She loved being in front of the camera,' I say to her boyfriend from all that time ago, who is showing me these three little films on his laptop. I must not allow myself to feel anything until later. I don't want to embarrass Adam, who has brought me these things I have asked to see.

I knew Adam would be up for it when I asked if I could tell his story. 'Yeah, sure,' he shrugged as if it were no big deal. In my collection I wanted to include someone who wasn't old and wasn't dead, and who had already demonstrated great courage and resilience in their young life. I have never met anyone quite like Adam, who combines such artistic, creative sensitivity with a core of steely strength and ambition. It is as if he accepts that life's setbacks can batter and wound, but he will not let them destroy him. He was similar to Rosa in that way.

His background was very different from hers however. His mum Linda was born in a suburb of Rugby and in Adam's nonchalant words, 'grew up with chavvy people.' Linda's father was a roofer whose drinking and irascibility increased when he fell off a roof and injured his back. He dominated his wife, he shouted at the dog; he would even yell at his daughter for 'colouring in too loudly'. Linda left school at sixteen and was a hairdresser before becoming an aerobics teacher. Adam's father also left school at sixteen and became an engineer. The parents separated when Adam was about five, his brother three.

His earliest memory is waking up for school, going into his mum and dad's bedroom and seeing that his mother wasn't there. He wandered around the house wondering where she was, until he noticed the spare room door was open and she was lying in bed there. 'Get your brother,' she said to him. Then she told them both that she and their dad were separating. She had met someone else at the sports centre where she worked. This man was Adam's stepfather for the next fifteen years, until the relationship ended – not long after Rosa died. I only met him once, outside the hospital where I had just identified Rosa in the chapel of rest. 'She was a one-off, that girl,' he said affectionately, and I knew exactly what he meant.

From the age of four Adam had loved playing games and messing about on computers. At school he was equally interested in science and art. 'I like learning how things work, and I'm good at doing things with my hands. Because I'm so logical, I don't see art as this "use your feelings" kind of thing. For me art is more of a science. I might ask myself, "how does this printer work?" and I have the same approach to art.' So he began studying how artists create certain effects, how a realistic portrait can be achieved. The A levels he chose were maths, physics and art. 'Anything,' he says, 'to avoid writing, because I'm pretty sure I'm dyslexic.'

When applying to university courses he decided architecture might combine both his drawing and practical skills. At his interview the tutor suggested interior architecture.

I interject, 'I'm not sure what that means exactly?'

Adam explains. 'When an architect designs a building they'll design it externally, decide how they want it to look and then fill it with floors and rooms, whereas an interior architect asks themselves "how will people want to use this space, how will they interact with it?" That interested me, rather than designing for the sake of something looking nice.'

And so he arrived at university on a sunny afternoon in September 2007. We were driving Rosa from a different direction, and left her there anxious about whether she would be all right, whether she would look after herself properly, hoping she would enjoy her course and make good friends. As soon as she had got rid of her fussing, nervous parents, Rosa went to find a bar that had a dance floor. Meanwhile Adam had made his way, with a friend of his from school and some people he had just met from his halls of residence, to the same student bar.

He began feeling restless, bored by his new acquaintances. 'I decided I was just going to leave them and go dance on my own. Funny, because it's out of character, it's not the sort of thing I do.' But something propelled him on to that dance floor. He was dancing and chatting to some people and suddenly a hand came out of nowhere and grabbed him, pulling him into a circle of students dancing close by.

It was Rosa.

They danced and danced, and later, when she and her new friends were leaving, she said 'do you want to come along?'

Rosa and Adam clicked instantly. 'She had such a big personality,' he says.

I tell Adam proudly that she was fun and irreverent even when she was little. She was a 'character'. I think it was something to do with the way her brain was wired, because of the epilepsy. The doctors referred to it as her 'disinhibition'. She never thought, 'Oh I'd better not say that,' she just said it.

Adam laughs in recognition. 'You never knew what she was going to come out with next!'

He pauses. '…I think because at one point she had been fat… she was like the fat girl in a thin girl's body. When you're fat and you think no one loves you, no one fancies you, you become that jokey, funny one.'

Yes, I agree. When you're not the pretty teenager you have to rely on your personality and get attention in other ways. Maybe that's why Rosa was always up for things. Even when she became very pretty – and she did – she retained the personality of the ugly friend, rather than the beautiful girl who gets a lot of attention and never needs to make an effort.

'I loved the fact that Rosa was driven, she was ambitious,' Adam continues. 'She was really fun. She was like the epitome of the first year at uni – that new, fresh, fun time when you're let loose into a new independent life, everything is heightened, good, exciting.' Two weeks into the term Adam went back home to break up with the school girlfriend he had left behind in Rugby. Apparently Rosa had told him in no uncertain terms, 'I really like you but you've got to decide what you want to do.'

But what about Rosa's dark side, I'm thinking. The epilepsy, the anorexia, the periods of depression that plagued her as a teenager. I wonder if she ever divulged any of this? Did it ever reveal itself?

'I remember being in her messy room and seeing a box of pills and asking what they were for. She didn't want to tell me, and then she blurted out that she had epilepsy. But you know, we never argued, only when I would get frustrated by her scattiness. I think *your* parental responsibility got passed on to me! I became to some extent the parent figure. There was always that hope I could train her out of it, but it was impossible. She had no common sense.'

'And she was stubborn,' I say.

I laugh as I tell Adam how 'anti-art' she had been until she went to university, and how surprised I was when she revealed a sudden enthusiasm for gallery visiting. That's when I knew she was in love. For years I had dragged her to countless art galleries and museums and she had always complained bitterly about it. I recount the story of our visit to Manchester when I had insisted on taking her and her sister to the City Art Gallery. I parked the two teenagers in front of Sam Taylor-Wood's short film of David Beckham sleeping, hoping that might be of interest, and was so pleased when I saw Rosa scribbling something in a book that had been left there for visitor feedback. When I looked, she had written 'I HATE ART' in enormous capitals, covering the whole page.

'And yet,' Adam says wistfully, 'she was always showing off... she would say proudly, "my mum took me to lots of art galleries."'

As if to impress him?

Adam remembers meeting us, Rosa's parents. It was only a few weeks into the term. Rosa had suggested an expensive French restaurant. 'I remember going to the restaurant with you. It was the first time I'd had snails. I think I'd expected from what Rosa had said that you'd be really posh... and then I thought when I met you, oh yes you're quite posh, because you're well spoken. But Andrew was so down to earth, super chatty. I thought, "these guys are lovely, nice people."'

And I, of course, remember meeting Adam. His asymmetrical haircut has been replaced by a shorter one, his features have matured and his gaucheness has gone, but it is still long, lean Adam, with his puckish face and the northern inflexions to his voice, who sits opposite me now at the kitchen table.

We talk about Rosa's relationship with her older sister Ellie, the way Rosa always longed to be like her – academic, pretty, popular. But then she would do infuriating things like steal Ellie's things and never admit she had done so, only for Ellie to spot her on Facebook, partying, wearing the very clothes she had denied taking.

'Rosa never thought about the consequences of anything,' Adam says.

'No she never did…' My voice breaks slightly. 'Her drinking used to make me so nervous. We were warned by the doctors that alcohol would interfere with the efficacy of the medication. And I knew she was drinking. It drove me to distraction because she wouldn't take responsibility for herself, though she did take her medicine…'

I pause looking to Adam for reassurance but he isn't responding. 'I hope?'

He shakes his head. 'She was terrible at that.'

'Oh, was she really?' I grimace. 'That's so frustrating, because if she'd taken the bloody medicine…'

'I know…'

'It's like the pill, you can't just take it on a Wednesday and think that will be fine. It's got to build up in the system. I would try and explain this to her a million times but she'd zone out.'

'I was exactly the same,' Adam says. 'I was always that parent asking, "Did you take your pills today?", "Why not?" Then she'd have a seizure and I'd ask her again, "Did you take the pills?", "No.", "Well, that's why you had a seizure!"'

Our voices are raised, talking quickly, interrupting each other.

'Yeah, drives you crazy!' I say this as if she is still alive, making us mad.

'I'd say to her, "*you* don't have to deal with it, it's me that has to."'

'Yeah!' I echo the sentiment, like a call and response. 'And surely you don't *want* to have the seizures?' I ask Rosa hypothetically. 'So why are you always pushing it?'

'To her it made no difference, she'd have the seizure, obviously she wouldn't remember it.'

'That's right!'

'...And then she'd be in bed for the next few hours. So I'd say, "Look – it's me that has to deal with it, has to suffer, so unless you want to put me through all that stress... just take your medicine!"'

We're getting very angry with her.

I say, 'Maybe if she'd taken more responsibility to take the medicine regularly, she wouldn't have had the seizure that terrible day... it's crazy-making!'

'Yes, yes, exactly!'

'Yeah, there we are, all left devastated,' I'm shouting now, 'and she's having fun in heaven or something... you just want to shake her!'

'It was always so frustrating!'

We both laugh bitterly.

Adam sounds thoughtful as he says, quietly now, 'Yes, absolutely, no consequences. I remember you telling me that she shouldn't drink, and I made a conscious effort to make sure she wouldn't ever get smashed, and sometimes I would have to take a drink off her because she didn't need it.'

And then he tells me a story that makes my blood run cold.

'She always had that need for acceptance. I remember I was in a club with her once, and some guys gave her some drugs...'

I make a whistling noise, then a slow intake of breath. 'Oh no...'

'And she came back from the toilet, and I said, "what the fuck have you just done?"'

My voice is almost a whisper now. 'But she always swore to me she never took drugs...'

'Well, she lied,' he bats back sharply, and then, seeing my expression, softens a little. 'I think it was only once.'

'Cocaine or something?'

'I think it was ecstasy.'

'Oh God,' I groan, 'that's just about the worst thing you can take if you have epilepsy!'

I don't know that actually, but I do know that ecstasy can induce a seizure in people who are not epileptic so what might it do to an epileptic brain. Surely the risks are astronomically higher?

Adam begins telling me about the night in the club when a boy Rosa knew gave her a bag of pills. I feel sick with dread, as if my daughter was still alive and I was filled with anxiety about the danger, the risk, at the outcome of the story.

'There was a boy on Rosa's course, a gay lad, I never liked. He always seemed a really bad influence and there were a couple of times I had to pull her away from him. This time he had given her a little bag of MDMA or something and she'd gone to the toilet and took the whole lot…'

'Oh no!' I feel ill thinking about it. I had told Adam at the beginning of our conversation that I was searching for the truth, but right now it would be more comforting to be fed lies or just be kept in the dark.

'I've never done it, but you're supposed to just take a little bit, and she took the whole lot.'

'That's terrible – she could have died!' I shout this out as if she isn't dead now anyway, as if the worst hasn't already happened. My awareness that her death at a young age was almost inevitable has come as a cruel realisation.

'And then what?'

'The guy who had given it to her was angry because she had taken the whole bag. I dragged Rosa home and she was off her face…' He rolls his head around in imitation. 'I said to her she was an idiot, I said, "Drugs are going to fuck with the chemicals in your head." I was so angry but she was so out of it she didn't know.'

'Well thank God she survived that…'

'Yeah…'

'She might not have done, you know.'

'I was so glad that I was there, because if she had just been out with them…'

'And thank God you were you, Adam, because she might have had a boyfriend who was also off his face or something.'

He nods, 'Yes, yeah, yeah…'

'She always had that wish to push it, push it…'

'Yes, it was almost like a denial. Like she didn't want to admit that she had epilepsy.'

'Yes, she wanted to test it, see how far she could go.'

'I think she always felt she wasn't normal, so whatever she could do to make herself feel normal, to fit in, she would just do, without thinking of the consequences.'

'Yes, she had no sense of personal responsibility. Oh Rosa!' I shout her name out in exasperation. 'And what about that friend of hers? I suppose he didn't know she had epilepsy…'

'He probably did,' interjects Adam.

'But as a mum… I don't understand… I just want to… how could he do this?'

Adam shakes his head.

We have been talking for a while and I need to eat. I turn away to heat some soup and with my back to him I call out a question.

'Tell me about when you left Oxford Brookes.'

'Well, meeting Lucie was the big thing,' he begins and I feel my heart lurching, because although I have known that he has been with Lucie for seven years, I find this unbearably, unreasonably painful. I remember that summer of 2008, after weeks of Adam staying with us following Rosa's death, taking him to the station and sitting with him in the car before his train arrived. He had looked broken, and I wanted to boost him up. 'Adam,' I had said, 'you're nineteen. Don't let this ruin everything. You will have other relationships, you have the whole of your life ahead of you.' I meant it very sincerely, and yet when I first heard that he was seriously involved with a new girlfriend, I felt sad and envious and fiercely loyal to Rosa. I couldn't bear it. Adam knew this, and for years avoided mentioning Lucie.

But I hide my feelings now. 'Oh, yes, tell me about that,' I say cheerfully, turning round. 'Was she at Oxford Brookes?'

'Yes, she was, in the year above.'

'Had you known her before?'

'After me and Rosa broke up... what am I saying, we didn't break up... That was the first time in my life that I was single. And that was weird for me because I had been in long-term relationships, first with my girlfriend at school for three years, then straight out of that into a relationship with Rosa for almost a year. So it was the first time I had been single and old enough to go "on the pull" sort of thing. I had never done that before.'

I have sat down again with the soup and various other things to eat. My smile belies the lump in my throat. Of course, he was a young student. Naturally he had to go on the pull. A flash of memory of Rosa and I sitting by the fire drinking tea when she was at home that December, what was to be her last Christmas. She was telling me about Adam. 'He's a "sticker". He doesn't seem to mind that I have epilepsy or anything.' She said it proudly. I remember feeling warmed by the fire and by the fact that Rosa and I were having this intimate chat because so often in the past our exchanges were angry and confrontational.

'It was weird,' Adam continues. 'I suppose when you're a bunch of lads you go out, looking for a girlfriend.'

'But did you feel in some way – I don't wish to put words in your mouth, maybe you didn't but... that you didn't want to fall in love because it had been so painful to lose someone you love?'

I realise I'm projecting, wanting him to feel this.

Adam stammers a bit, trying to formulate his thoughts. He tells me about a girl called Rachel who moved into his student house. Because she didn't really know anyone, Adam made an effort to be friendly to her and it was nice to have a good friend who was a girl. 'Because Rosa had been my best friend, so it was therapeutic to have someone to fill that role.'

They hung out together and became really close. But one day she said, 'I feel that you fancy me and I don't feel the same way,' and then was upset when Adam told her that no, he only wanted her as a good friend. 'I don't think she had ever had that. Rachel was beautiful and I don't think she had ever had a strong friendship with a boy that wasn't sexual as well.' Soon after, Rachel got a boyfriend and didn't speak to Adam much anymore. 'It's sad,' he says. 'I realised that for seven years I had always had a female figure in my life, whether that was a friend or a girlfriend.'

He began searching for this person to fill the gap, going out all the time, getting together with different girls. 'It became a bit relentless.'

Then he met Lucie. 'I met her in this club. We got on super well. I remember walking back to her place that evening and we started to kiss and stuff and then before it went any further I said, I've got to go. I felt "this is someone I actually really like", but then Rosa just popped into my head and I knew I had to leave. I went home and burst into tears. The next day I explained to her what had happened, why I had acted like this. And we went for coffee or something...'

He tells me it was nice to find someone who wasn't at all like Rosa. 'Lucie is very calm. She is a very shy person. Until you get to know her, and then she's really fun.'

I feel the unreasonable squeeze of the heart again.

'So where Rosa was massively outgoing,' he continues, 'Lucie was the opposite. And I thought that was nice, because she doesn't remind me of Rosa all the time which was exactly what I needed.'

'That's good. So you weren't comparing them.'

'Yes, I remember the first proper date and she was so shy, she was hardly talking.'

'Yeah!' I laugh, 'Because Rosa never stopped talking!'

'Yes, there were almost awkward silences but I managed to keep the conversation going. So it evolved from there...'

'Now it's been going about seven years, hasn't it?'

'Yes, it was seven years in December.'

I wonder out loud what Lucie's feelings might be about what happened with Rosa.

'She understands that Rosa meant a lot to me,' he answers.

There is a pause as we carry on eating our lunch. And then I find myself apologising again for a truly bad thing that I did when Lucie and Adam got together.

'I'm so sorry, you know, about that terrible thing I did.'

Adam nods. He knows exactly what I am referring to.

I try to explain. 'I had these moments when I thought I would go insane with the grief of it all. It was overwhelming. And the problem with grief is that you are in that moment when the other bereaved person – or someone else – isn't in the moment. It's very hard to find the times when you can talk about it and be supported and supportive. Andrew and I...'

'What are these?' Adam interrupts, pointing to the various dips I have placed on the kitchen table. Would he rather I didn't talk about this anymore?

'That's beetroot, this one is mint, that's butternut squash I think.' He doesn't look very keen.

'...Andrew and I found it hard to share times when we could be supportive of each other. So I would have these private moments when I would be a bit obsessive and sit and watch that little film you made on holiday of Rosa in a bikini mixing a cocktail, or I would go rather manically on Facebook because I still had her login details. They were registered on my computer at home and it was logged in all the time. I would go to my computer and look, pathetically, at what her friends were doing, hoping they had left a message saying they missed her. It was a way of connecting with her, of still being part of ongoing lives associated with her.'

I was on Rosa's Facebook page when I saw a conversation between Adam and Lucie that made it clear these two were in a serious, loving relationship. It was six months after Rosa had died and I felt the most unimaginable pain, as if my daughter's life had meant nothing, as if she was already replaced. And with the grief came the overwhelming rage, the 'it should have been her', scream. Before I thought through what I was doing I had posted 'Don't you think it's a bit soon to fall in love again?' on the stream of their conversation, and pressed 'Done' or 'Send' or whatever it is.

Instantly I panicked. I knew it would come through to Adam as a message from Rosa, his dead girlfriend, with photo of her attached. But I was frozen in front of my computer. I seemed incapable of doing anything to put it right.

After a sleepless night I sent Adam a text. 'I'm so, so sorry, I'm so ashamed.'

He was understandably furious and upset. 'That was terrible. You don't know what I've been through,' he texted back. I kept apologising because I was truly, deeply sorry and ashamed.

And once again, I am apologising.

'I shouldn't have been looking at your private messages. But I was in this weird state of needing a connection with Rosa, and seeing what I saw... the grief was overwhelming... it felt as if everyone was moving on and I was stuck, it was like, "Rosa is gone, and I want everyone still to be grieving for her." Without even thinking I did that, in this mad way, it wasn't premeditated, it was a reaction...'

And then I tell him how I hadn't slept that night, imagining him suddenly getting this message out of the blue – from Rosa.

Adam hasn't said anything yet.

'I actually felt dizzy,' I continue, 'and physically sick. And mortified. But it took me hours and hours to pluck up the courage to confess and say how sorry I was. It was like when you have done something terrible when you're little and not being able to tell your parents. It was awful, and I can't imagine how terrible that must have been for you.'

'It was so freaky...'

'I'm so sorry.'

'...I'm not religious, I don't believe in anything superstitious. Anything supernatural I think is nonsense. I can understand why some people believe in it but I'm from a science background, those sort of things don't make sense to me. And then that happened and I was...'

He pauses. 'I can't even describe the feeling, it was almost like someone had found out something you never wanted them to know, and now the world knows. A wave of fear came over me, I kept thinking, "I don't understand how this could have happened." There was no logical answer for it. I felt so sick.'

He then tells me it made him question the relationship he was in, asking himself whether he was doing the right thing. He suddenly felt really guilty about meeting Lucie.

I am so repentant, contrite. Chastened. It is my turn to be silent.

'I remember just not knowing what to do?' He throws this out like a question.

'Did you tell Lucie?'

'No, no, I didn't tell anyone for a while. I didn't sleep that night either. It brought everything back.'

'So at what point did you think it must have been mad Vanessa? Did you think, "Oh, that bitch of a mother!"'

'No, because I didn't know it was you. It could have been Andrew, Ellie, you...'

I interrupt quickly. 'Andrew or Ellie would *never* do anything like that. And looking back, it is incomprehensible that I would do that to you either. It shows what forms grief can take. I had told you to move on with your life. You were so young. But on the other hand I couldn't bear it when you did. You know, I tell people this story. They are so appalled. It's almost like a confessional, I have to test my friends: "Look, I'm going to tell you something I did that was so awful, will you still be my friend now?"'

Adam laughs. He says something kind about how he understands. 'There was no need to hold it against you. I know you were upset.'

'Yes, when one feels that bad, you don't think it through. I think I felt you didn't love Rosa anymore because you had transferred your love to someone else.'

Adam smiles. 'You'd done a "Rosa"! You jumped in without thinking of the consequences.'

'Exactly.'

'That's where she got it from!' Adam laughs again. I join in, but then become more thoughtful.

'Actually, I do share the recklessness that Rosa had. When I write, I need to say things that maybe I shouldn't give a voice to, things I should not "share". But at some level I don't want to be sensible and careful, I want people to know how it feels.'

Yes, I want to bring the feelings up from the basement. Expose, remind, confront. It is risky.

Adam is quiet now. We have come to the end of that part of the conversation. I hope he has truly forgiven me.

* * *

When Adam left university in 2009 he lived for a while with Lucie in Shepherds Bush. It was a miserable place with a horrible landlady and they hated being there. While Lucie went out to work, Adam made bits of money through online betting and designing computer games. This led him to 'modding Xboxes' and selling them on. I feel a generational chasm opening between us as he tells me about this. I don't really understand what 'modding' or even 'Xboxes' are, but I guess – with some help from Wikipedia – that it's something to do with modifying the built-in hardware and security mechanisms of video game consoles.

Adam really wanted to go into architectural visualisation, making 3D models, but despite sending out endless CVs to architectural firms, he was getting no response. One day a customer who had brought an Xbox for Adam to modify mentioned that he worked for a place that hired out graffiti artists for murals and workshops. When Adam showed some interest and produced his portfolio, the man was impressed. 'Could you do that on a wall?' he asked.

A couple of weeks later Adam's phone rang and it was the same guy, asking him to design a website. When soon after, a new company was formed by some of the employees called Graffiti Life, he was told 'we can't offer you a wage but you can be part of it, and own shares in the company'. Adam took over the social media side, specialising in digital marketing and design, but also began learning the techniques of drawing on walls. He picked it up very quickly.

The company was slowly growing and expanding but Adam was unable to take a wage for about two years. This was a big strain on his relationship. 'I *knew* we were going to be successful because I could see the rate we were growing. I could understand why Lucie was worried, she was saying, "Well if you're doing so well, why haven't you got anything to show for it," but everything we were earning was being put back into the company. We knew we had a great product that people would want, but people didn't know they wanted it.'

The popularity and fame of Banksy came at a fortuitous time. 'It made graffiti a familiar thing, rather than something niche that only subcultures like. So we were around at the right time, because people want "cool", and are willing to pay for "cool".'

Graffiti Life markets its artists as 'fine mural painters', able to recreate any image on to any surface. They have gone from a garage in a grim suburb of south London to an office in a fashionable part of the East End and are now taking projects all over the world, handling commissions from well-known publications and television shows. They have worked on advertising campaigns for well-known brands and last year helped promote three major movies and organise team-building graffiti workshops for companies. Subculture has become something the establishment will pay good money for. Their work adorns everything from urban walls to cars. One customer even commissioned an image of Beethoven to be reproduced on his piano.

Success has brought new possibilities. Adam and Lucie have moved out of the miserable flat in Shepherd's Bush and live in an up-and-coming area of east London. They like to travel and eat in nice restaurants. A few months ago I noticed that Adam had befriended me on Facebook, where I sometimes read about the latest developments of Graffiti Life. I notice that he has posted a sequence of small films of him and Lucie on their latest trip to New York and more recently to Naples.

I don't think I will look at them yet though. It would be too painful.

Luisa

I'M IN ONE OF THE MOST BEAUTIFUL CITIES OF THE WORLD. It's sunny and warm. At home in England I have left behind a secure and apparently enviable life. I have everything I could wish for. I am lucky.

I want to be dead.

I thought I'd stopped wanting to be dead.

I thought I'd laid the ghosts to rest, buried the demons. I thought I'd understood it all, cleared the paths of thorns, made sense of the clichés and found a way out. But I can't bear to look ahead and I've done the looking back. I inhabit a no man's land: a territory where there is neither past nor future.

I feel I don't exist, that I am not truly present.

'I, I, I,' these sentences begin, as if I want to reaffirm my reality.

I'm floating off somewhere.

Come back then.

What am I feeling, seeing, hearing right now? Heat. Shutters open to let in a small breeze. Outside the sound of labourers on a nearby building site, church bells, loud Italian voices coming up from the street. Inside, facing my bed are exhibition posters from the 1980s stuck to a wardrobe. This room used to be my mother's office and she has made it clear that nothing must be changed.

Stop. I'm travelling into the past again.

The wardrobe door is slightly open. A linen jacket that hasn't been hung properly is about to fall off.

Downstairs my mother rests. I tried to take her out today to meet an old friend and relative by marriage she has not seen for several years. Luisa expressed pleasure when I first mentioned a possible meeting.

'Bridget is coming to Florence,' I had said on my last visit.

'Oh! Such a nice woman.'

'Yes, isn't she? She would love to see you.'

Luisa smiled.

A week ago I wrote from England reminding her of my arrival and telling her how much Bridget was looking forward to meeting up. I followed this with a telephone call explaining the same thing. Luisa is in her mid-nineties and forgetful and does not like surprises. On the morning of the meeting I speak to Bridget on the telephone to confirm the appointment.

'Welcome to Florence! Let's meet at 3 p.m. in Robiglio, the famous cafe in Via dei Servi.'

'Perfect,' Bridget says.

Luisa and I are having coffee after lunch.

'Why don't you have a rest for an hour or so and I shall get you up at 2.30 so you can meet Bridget,' I suggest.

'Who?'

'Bridget Sackville-West.'

'Oh yes, nice woman.'

At 2.30 p.m. I am trying to wake my mother. She is lying on a bare mattress under a blanket because this morning I insisted on washing the sheets. They only get washed when I come to stay because Luisa refuses to have any domestic help from outside. The only sheets she will allow me to put on the bed are the pair of clashing nylon ones she likes – one yellow, one pink – despite having cupboards full of beautiful white linen embroidered with her mother's initials.

'It's time to wake up!'

She looks dead. No, it's me that wants to be dead. Or do I want her to be dead. No, I want her to be alive but energetic and difficult and bossy, like she used to be. It is she who used to come into my room in the holidays, furious that I was still lying around, sleeping in, instead of up and about, achieving things.

I shake her arm but she does not budge. Maybe she really is dead. No, pull yourself together.

'Mummy!' I shout.

Her eyes open very wide. She looks terrified.

'We are meeting Bridget, remember?'

'Who?'

'Bridget. She will be in Robiglio at 3 p.m.'

'*Ah! Si...*' she answers in Italian.

I try and help her up, but she pushes me away. Under that blanket she is wearing all her clothes, the only clothes I have seen her in during the last year or so. A thick, warm grey jumper, a long greyish-blue skirt done up with safety pins because she has lost so much weight. Flesh-coloured tights, a stained white blouse, a filthy orange scarf. I feel so sad about that scarf because I remember it new and elegantly tied around her neck to complement a smart suit she wore in the 1970s.

Underneath all the winter clothes I know there are layers, made up of a petticoat and vests. Outside the city bakes in thirty-five-degree heat and I am sweating in linen.

She has to go to the bathroom.

'Of course,' I say.

I wait, sitting in the hall by the telephone, worrying that time is running out and that we shall be late arriving at the cafe. I wonder if I should tell her that I must go ahead, I must let Bridget know. I get up from the chair and walk to the bathroom but the door is closed, unwelcoming. She has been there now for twenty minutes. I pace around and finally Luisa comes out and begins putting her coat on.

'It's really very warm, I don't think you'll need that.'

'Ah.' The coat is returned to the coat stand.

We have an argument about keys. These are yours, no they are mine, no they are yours, you took these, no I didn't. Eventually we begin to walk down the stairs. It is well past 3 p.m.

'I'm going to run ahead,' I say, 'Bridget will be wondering where we are.'

'Who?'

'Bridget.' I sigh.

'Ah si.'

I sprint across the square and then spot Bridget over the road from Robiglio, looking fresh in summer clothes. Bridget is in her eighties but looks a generation younger than Luisa. She waves cheerfully and seeing her friendly, expectant face makes me want to cry. I smile and we embrace.

We sit on the low wall of the Renaissance house opposite Robiglio and I explain. Luisa is slow, I'm so sorry she is late, she seems tired today. What I want to say is I can't do this anymore, she won't allow me to get any help, not even a doctor and I feel sad all the time and I don't know what to do, where to go next. I hint at some of this but don't say that I want to be dead. Of course I don't say that.

One isn't allowed to say that.

Bridget suggests that we walk back across the square towards Luisa's apartment to see what has become of her.

'There she is!' she says, spotting a hunched figure in the distance. I see a little old lady dressed in grey wool on this baking day, hobbling along with a stick. She looks like the old Befana who visits children on 6 January, flying around from home to home on her broomstick. If they are good they get sweets and toys in their little sacks, but if they've been naughty they only find sweet coal, like I did that time when I was seven and my little American friend Julie was upset for me.

We reach Luisa who stops as we approach. She hardly acknowledges Bridget but begins lecturing us on the equestrian monument in the middle of the square. She may not remember much about today but she knows all about Ferdinando de' Medici on his horse.

She was an art historian after all. That is why my father loved her.

We are in Robiglio waiting for our drinks. The order takes time because Luisa does not know what she wants. 'You choose,' she says to the young waiter, but every time he suggests something she shakes her head.

'Why would I want a coffee? It is too hot.'

'An orange juice perhaps? Freshly squeezed?'

'Orange juice? I never drink orange juice!' she says, as if the waiter is an idiot and should be well aware of that.

'Iced tea?'

Luisa makes a face and then her face softens. 'How old are you?' He looks slightly taken aback and is about to answer but she interrupts. 'I was born in 1920! Can you work out how old I am?'

The waiter looks flummoxed.

'Do you know who that is?' She points at Ferdinando on his bronze horse, changing the subject again.

I'm hot, embarrassed, thirsty. Bridget has not said anything.

'Umm, not sure…' the waiter smiles awkwardly.

'Mummy, the order,' I say, bringing her back. 'What would you like?'

'Who do you think Ferdinando de' Medici is looking at?'

We all look at the Grand-Duke as if he will give us the answer.

'I think a lady has caught his eye. You see him looking to his right as if she is at the window of the Palazzo on the corner.'

The waiter smiles indulgently. 'Yes, um, Signora, your drink?'

'And the horse, you see he is facing ahead. It's very clever.'

'An apple juice would be great, thank you,' I smile stiffly.

Bridget is about to say something but Luisa interrupts.

'Those awful tourists! Poor Florence!' She is shaking her head.

The drinks arrive. Coffee for Bridget and me, a fizzy apple juice that Luisa will leave untouched on the table to attract the wasps and flies. A small plate of little homemade delicacies that I start gobbling up as if they will feed some emotional emptiness inside me.

Bridget and I make an attempt at conversation but Luisa is still looking vacantly over our heads to the low wall that Bridget and I were sitting on only ten minutes earlier.

'Just *look* at those tourists!' she says again.

We swivel our heads and see a couple resting their feet, checking something in their guidebook.

'Povera Firenze!'

I'm on edge, alert, as if I might suddenly be called upon to intervene. Am I simply worried by what Luisa might say next? That she may utter something racist I have heard from her before about the Chinese tourists I know she thinks are taking over the city? Or about the size of the American girls walking loudly past us? 'But their bottoms, Vanessa, their bottoms, how do they get such big bottoms?' Or about the Nigerian man hopelessly trying to sell his cheap umbrellas on such a hot day? Or the gypsy woman I've noticed begging with a baby in her arms? 'They're rich really you know, they are dropped off in the mornings by men driving a Mercedes and they relieve themselves in the square and pinch their babies to make you think they are hungry...'

The last time I came to this cafe it was winter two and a half years ago. I had met Luisa's youngest cousin Elena there, and we sat indoors at a table covered in a peach-coloured tablecloth, drinking tea and eating pastries. I hadn't seen her for twenty-five years. Zia Elena as I called her (Aunt Elena) had always been my favourite Italian relative, the least bourgeois. She was beautiful when young, with deep brown eyes and a gamine haircut like Audrey Hepburn, and had fallen in love with a handsome Swiss artist who after their marriage and the birth of two children betrayed her by running off with a life model. Elena selflessly devoted herself to a disabled son, and with so many troubles of her own always put others first. It was Elena, not Luisa's mother, who had come to London to support Luisa when I was about to be born. It was Elena who rushed to Sicily after her marriage broke up in order to help people made homeless in the aftermath of a terrible earthquake. There she met and later lived with a Sicilian man from 'peasant' stock called Pasquale who none of her relatives could relate to and were slow to accept as her partner. When I wrote to her twenty-eight years ago to tell that I had named my first baby after her she had answered, sounding pleased and incredulous, '"Elena" like me? Not spelt the English way?'

No, not the English way.

I had got in touch with Zia Elena two years ago after Luisa had a bad fall and was in hospital. It was miraculous that she had survived at all. Luisa's life was saved by a neighbour whose rooms overlooked the bedroom window, across an internal courtyard. He was closing the shutters when he saw her collapsed on her bedroom floor. The fire brigade had to break in her front door before the ambulance men could rush her to hospital. I arrived in Florence to find her bedroom like the aftermath of a massacre, an abandoned crime scene with furniture overturned and blood smeared over floor and walls. I cleaned for several hours, rushing to the bathroom at regular intervals to vomit and change the bloody water in the bucket. The mop was so encrusted with blood that I had to throw it away.

When I went downstairs to the floor below to get the key back from Signor Lotti, another neighbour, he had said, 'my son suggested we leave her to die.' I looked at him as if he had hit me in the stomach. His words made me physically flinch. What a strange and insensitive thing to say to a daughter about her mother, I thought, especially as he was aware that only a few years earlier I had lost a child. I knew the son hadn't forgiven Luisa for disputing a bill submitted after he had completed some redecorating work in her flat, but still. What flinty hearts!

It is a strange condominium, six apartments in all, inhabited by people I have known for years. In the 1970s Luisa was the one they came to when letters to the administrator or other such things needed to be written. She was the educated one, happy to articulate the concerns of everyone in the building. She was good at getting things done. We would laugh together about the various characters: the elderly lady on the ground floor who gave in to jealous rages over her ninety-year-old husband's 'flirting' with the eighty-five-year-old next door. Or the distracted professor who went to Paris forgetting he had left his bath taps running and caused a flood. Or the single mum who invited her 'young lover' to live with her – Luisa still refers to him as the woman's 'young lover' even though he has lived in the apartment next door for over twenty years, surviving his partner, who recently died of cancer in her fifties. Luisa would also tell me the story about Signor Lotti as a young man, spotting his future wife at the window of a Florentine orphanage – or was it a convent? – and conducting his whole courtship with his neck strained upwards to better see her. 'He can't have got a very good look,' she would laugh, 'because she always *was* terribly plain.'

She and Lotti used to get on before the fall-out over the son's decorating. At the time of Luisa's fall I simply didn't respond to his insensitive remark about 'leaving her to die', but took the door key in silence and resolved to avoid him as much as possible in future. Now they are civil to each other and she seems to have forgotten their previous disagreements.

The month's stay in hospital marked the beginning of Luisa's decline. She hated it. She shouted at the nurses, she despised the other patients. I would find her sitting in the day room holding her head in her hands, refusing to eat the meals brought to her. She distrusted the doctors and pleaded with them to let her go home, alternating anger and threats with pathetic whining. I brought her a new Marks and Spencer's nightie from England but when I presented it to her in the hospital she threw it back at me. 'I don't need this!' she shouted angrily as I tried to point out that really she shouldn't be wearing the charity clothes collected by nuns when she was probably more affluent than all the other old ladies put together.

When I did get Luisa home I pressed her to accept a carer but she refused. 'Elena can come. Elena looks after people.' I knew that wasn't fair. Elena was in her eighties and in any case she was busy looking after her older sister Vannozza who suffers from dementia. But Elena did visit Luisa, and one day she and I arranged to meet in Robiglio. In between sipping tea she told me then that Luisa was greatly loved by her family but that she had always been a difficult character.

'She is so clever, you see,' she said, as if this exonerated her from any bad behaviour.

At first I insisted on arranging care but the women sent by the agency never lasted more than a few weeks. Luisa argued and sacked every one or barricaded herself in her apartment so they couldn't get in. 'I can't bear to have anyone in the house,' she said.

There was one carer I particularly liked and I tried to warn her of Luisa's challenging behaviour.

'I can handle anything, Signora,' Maria-Rosa said proudly. 'I've never failed with anyone. The agency always give me the most difficult cases!' We both laughed. 'In fact I have so many amazing stories about the old people I have looked after over the years. Some are such interesting characters. People don't believe me, but I really love my job. I even like the cleaning!'

'You should write the stories down,' I suggested once.

'But I can't write...'

'You can tell me the stories if you like.'

We agreed that the next time I came to Florence I would bring a tape recorder and would write her stories up for her.

'And then I could print them all out for you and you could keep them in a folder or something.'

'Really? Like my own book?' She beamed.

A few weeks later I got a call from Maria-Rosa as I was waiting for a train on a rainy London platform. She was sobbing.

'Your mother has kicked me out... she was so angry... she wouldn't listen... this has never happened to me before.'

'I'm so sorry... what went wrong?'

'I was cleaning the kitchen,' she spluttered between sobs, 'and I put the medicine to one side... and...'

I couldn't hear any more for the sound of her crying, and then the line went dead.

For a while Luisa had no one to care for her, not even a doctor to keep an eye out. Now a woman comes a couple of times a week for an hour, and I have also registered her with a doctor whom she never consults. She hates the carer and refers to her as 'Mussolini'. I suspect the bad feeling is mutual and have given up trying to impose more help. But I worry because she self-medicates with Warfarin ('it makes me feel better'), buying it for a huge price from a pharmacist who turns a blind eye to the fact that her medical demands never come with a prescription.

And Zia Elena has disappeared from our lives once more.

At Robiglio we have finished our drinks. Luisa is flagging and I sense Bridget is getting restless. I go into the cafe to pay the bill and leave a large tip. The three of us make our way very slowly back across the square as Luisa repetitively complains about the uneven pavement. We pass the monument to Ferdinando de' Medici and when we arrive in front of the church Luisa says she is going home and she begins shuffling round the corner without saying a proper goodbye to Bridget. It doesn't matter. Bridget is kind and, as always, understands.

'I think she had had enough, don't you?' she smiles.

We speak a bit more about this and that before we agree to part. 'One thing I realise,' Bridget says, briefly returning to the subject. 'Luisa didn't really listen to anything we said, did she?'

No, she doesn't listen. She never really has.

I go upstairs to my room under the roof and lie on the hard single bed, feeling exhausted. Really it hasn't been a particularly bad or different day so why do I feel so depressed? I list all the things that should make me grateful and contented – my daughter, my husband, my good friends, my opportunities. It is a privileged life I lead. I fight that creeping 'I want to be dead' feeling but I have had it for weeks, months, years even. I tried to describe it to a friend once as 'having treacle in the veins', as if I were regularly injected with some sticky substance clogging up pathways of energy. That combined with desperation for the sensation to end. But nothing seems to shift it until it decides to shift itself.

Later that evening I prepare supper. When I call Luisa to the kitchen she says, 'I have eaten already but I shall keep you company.'

I know she hasn't eaten anything and I am pleased when she picks at the salads I have laid out on the table. She tells me a story about remembering me sharing a pram with her sister Nori while she – the older toddler – walked alongside. I have heard different versions of this story many times.

'That's not possible,' I say, knowing I should not contradict her, knowing this will confuse and upset her.

'Yes, you were both babies,' she answers, 'You don't remember because you were so young.'

'Don't be ridiculous,' I snap back cruelly. 'Of course I wasn't a baby in 1921! The other baby in the pram was your cousin Anna.'

'Oh,' she says looking muddled. She has been rhythmically scratching the tip of her nose all evening and it looks red and sore.

'Is there something wrong with your nose?' I say, meaning my voice to sound gentle and concerned, wishing to help, to suggest the application of a medicated cream or something to make it better. But I feel my nerves jangling and the question comes out harshly, like an accusation.

As we finish supper Luisa asks if I would help her wash her hair. We go to the bathroom and she unpicks the clips that are holding the thinning strands in place before bending her head forward into the bath. I notice the hump at the top of her back, the skin of her thin arms flapping away from the bones. The taps are stiff and rusty from underuse, the water a trickle from the old shower attachment. It takes me a while to get the temperature right. At the side of the bath sits the female figure I made in pottery class when I was twelve and gave to Luisa for Christmas. We always referred to her as 'The Mermaid' even though she clearly has two legs. This was probably because she was placed in the bathroom surrounded by the shells and the flat-shaped stones Luisa and I collected together over summer breaks on the Tuscan coast when I was a child, moments of normality before I was left with Ben or with relatives or at the children's summer camp La Corallina that I hated because I was not a name there but a number I will never forget.

I remember the green swimming costume my mother had, and how beautiful she was then, and the red toenails, and the sixties summer shift dresses and strappy sandals and the large white-and-blue beach bag with an anchor on it that the shells would disappear into, to be taken back to Florence with the rest of her luggage. There were times I managed to persuade her to buy a few impressive conch shells to add to the collection, as well as the large starfish and those with wonderful names like King's Crown and Bleeding Tooth. On my birthday she gave me a book about shells to look them up. I have it still.

The shells are dusty now and streaked with dirt. I resolve to wash them tomorrow, to get a bucket of water to put them all in and see their faded colours restored to their natural brightness. But I must bring myself back to the task in hand. Luisa is waiting. What a strange mix of tenderness and revulsion fills my heart as I shampoo and massage the creamy substance into her scalp. I need to rinse her hair several times before the water stops running black.

'Again, again,' she says as I move my hands across her head, and this reminds me of when my children were very young and they would say that to me after I did something that made them feel joyful.

Ben

On Sunday 18 January 1970 a documentary on Virginia Woolf, *A Night's Darkness, A Day's Sail*, was broadcast by the BBC. It presented the character and work of the writer seen through the recollections of those who had known her. I was thirteen and at boarding school and had little interest then in either Virginia Woolf or her associates, but my excitement at the prospect of seeing my father on the TV overrode any indifference to the subject. Back then there was no possibility of recording programmes and watching them later, so I was given special permission to go to matron's room an hour after lights out and wait for the documentary to begin. It was late in the evening, shortly after the beginning of term, and I sat in my pyjamas waiting in anticipation. Matron was impressed that my father was to be on the television though equally indifferent to Virginia Woolf, so she left me alone, but not before bringing me hot chocolate and biscuits as a special treat.

Leonard Woolf was first to come on the screen, looking frail and old. This was followed by a long shot of a choppy sea as the credits rolled and a well-spoken voice read a passage from *To the Lighthouse*. Ben appeared on a couple of occasions, first on his own and then with his younger brother, my uncle Nigel. During the final part of the programme I was restless, wondering if there would be any more of my father. By now I was bored, as the moment of recognition and excitement at seeing him framed by the television had passed. The hot drink and biscuits had been consumed and I wanted to go to bed.

Thirteen years later, aged twenty-three, I had left Ben's rented flat for a house in north London. One Saturday morning I noticed in the TV listings that the same programme on Virginia Woolf was being aired at 2.30 p.m. Again, the excitement mounted as I prepared to watch because I was going to see Ben – who had died so suddenly a couple of years previously – return to life. Again I watched alone, but this time I was crying within a minute of seeing my father move and speak. I hadn't been able to say goodbye, I missed him, and here he was reminding me of all the elements that had made him unique and rendered me bereft.

Recently I watched him for a third time. It was shortly after I had seen Rosa come alive in the little films her boyfriend Adam had shown me, and that ache of longing to see those I had lost returned. How lucky we are now, I thought, to be able to revisit loved ones this way. There is so much more to gain from the moving image than from the flatness of a photograph. Even if they can't see us we can meet their three-dimensional selves, we can hear their voices and see their movements, and for a few minutes relive a time that has passed.

In my memory, Ben always looked the same. Perhaps because I only knew him for twenty years, from his early forties to early sixties, he seemed perpetually stuck in middle age. And Rosa, who died at nineteen, would still look like a young woman if she were alive now, aged twenty-seven. It feels strange that I shall always remember my father and my daughter the way they were when they died. I shall never know them older.

When in the early 1980s I had set the video in order to record the repeat, I had intended it to capture my father forever. But despite keeping the cassette, I had never watched the documentary again. It was enough to know a living version of my father was there on a shelf in my house, trapped in the box. Taken prisoner. Now so much time had passed and I worried how I would get it to work.

Would the video recorder, which I still kept in a cupboard, be too old to function? Would I have to get the film transferred on to DVD or a memory stick or something technically beyond me?

To my amazement, it came up instantly on YouTube, after I searched the title with little hope of finding it that way. And so I watched, intrigued. How slow moving and ponderous the documentary seems now. The pace was so gentle, the accents a caricature of a time long gone, the style of filming similarly outmoded, but all rather comforting for that. This time I was writing about Ben and I wanted to concentrate on what he had to say and how he was saying it: to get to the essence of his character and to watch as dispassionately as possible.

And there he was again, my eccentric, rumpled, loveable father, searching for the right word in his deep, hesitant voice. Then he was loping in baggy brown clothes through the gardens at Sissinghurst alongside his dashing and elegant brother.

Ben holds a book – one by Virginia I presume – looking grave, uncomfortable in comparison to Nigel, who, debonair in his steely blue suit, white shirt and tie, a flower in his lapel, exudes confidence and entitlement. (So different from the elderly uncle I remember from years later, walking around the same garden in his stained linen jacket and woolly jumper unravelling at the cuffs.)

I peer at the screen. Ben and Nigel have sat down on garden chairs. Ben is covering his mouth, in thought. The camera pans to Nigel who is describing Virginia talking to the two brothers when they were boys.

'She said to me:' Nigel begins, '"Now tell me what happened today?" and I said, "Well nothing, I've just come home from school and here I am," and she said, "No, no, no, that's no good, start from the beginning. What woke you up?" And I thought and I said, "Well it was the sun coming through my window at school." And then she leant forward and said, "What sort of sun? Was it a gentle sun or an angry sun?" And so from that we went on, and it was really a sort of game, but it also was a lesson in observation...'

A voice can be heard, interrupting Nigel's flow. The camera moves across to Ben's face. 'I don't think you've remembered this story...'

'I promise you I have!' Nigel laughs and crosses his arms defensively.

'I think you're muddling it up with another story.'

'No, it's absolutely vivid to me, because it was then that I began to understand what Virginia's work was all about for the first time. It's really an observation of human character...'

Ben interrupts again, shaking his hand. 'She wasn't very good at that.'

Nigel responds quickly. 'She was very good at the way character is expressed in gesture, dress, possessions, behaviour, all that sort of thing.'

'So long as she was able to create complete fantasy.'

The camera moves on and they do not appear again.

Here is Ben's journal on 14 January 1970, four days before the documentary was broadcast.

> To the preview of the Virginia Woolf film. It is marvellous, but also funny and lively. Full romance is made of the actual Cornish lighthouse. The musical accompaniment impeccable. Never too tragic or too sentimental. We sat with all the participants in the film, and to hear those Bloomsbury voices behind me, it was like being back in Fitzroy Square in 1909. Only Virginia's absence was felt. Just think in 100 years' time how interesting this will be! As though we had a film of all Charlotte Bronte's friends, recalling their memories of her.
>
> It was as if they had a 'stand-in' for me, an elderly bald crow who kept passing his fingers across his face, who spoke laboriously

in a broken voice. It bore some resemblance to a preposterous imitation of me by Philip. The experience was fairly appalling. But I was cheered up by being told, at the party afterwards, that what we see, hear or understand of ourselves bears not the slightest resemblance to the 'truth'.

In this case I disagree. For me the mannerisms revealed in the film were characteristic of my father: the earnest look, the laboured speech, the search to find the right word and expression, the gestures to give emphasis. The desire above all else to get to the core of things.

At this point in his life Ben was in his mid-fifties and had been beguiled by Simon, a very different character from David, the man he had loved thirty years earlier. A few days after he noted his thoughts on the Virginia Woolf documentary, and the nature of truth and character, Ben writes about Simon. 'I told him I was no longer in love with him in the way I was this time last year, but that I loved him more than anyone in the world. He knows me by now well enough to realise that *I am incapable of telling anything but the truth*.' (My italics.)

Indeed, and this was a trait that would occasionally upset me, for he could be insensitively blunt when giving his honest opinion to anything I asked him about. I remember annihilating negative replies to my pleas for reassurance about a drawing or a story I had produced, a new outfit I was wearing or a boyfriend I had introduced him to. If he didn't like something or someone he would say so. But when he did respond positively, it made it all the more rewarding, because I knew he meant it and it wasn't empty praise.

Shortly after writing these words on Ben I am at a book launch. I notice a very old man sitting in an armchair in the corner of the room and recognise him as Jeremy Hutchinson, a noted QC who in his time defended some of the most notorious cases brought to court: obscenity trials, political scandals, cases involving art forgery and drug trafficking. As young men he and Ben had been great friends. They had shared 'digs' in Oxford and corresponded for many years after leaving university. A decade ago I had shown Jeremy the letters he had written to my father, letters that Ben had always kept. Jeremy then produced the ones he had received in return, and insisted I keep them all so that I would have the complete set.

I cross the room where the party is in full swing, and lean down to congratulate Jeremy on his forthcoming 101st birthday. We only meet every couple of years, but whenever he sees me, my presence triggers an affectionate memory of Ben from their student days in the 1930s, and his face lights up.

'Hello!' he greets me, as always responding with warmth, smiling and indicating the chair beside him for me to sit on. And then, he says more wistfully, 'Oh Ben,' as if to himself or to the absent friend.

I make myself comfortable and Jeremy continues. 'He was *such* a character. Whenever he recounted a story to others about something we had done together or that I had witnessed, he would elaborate and embroider. "But it wasn't like that at all!" I would shout, and all of us would laugh, including Ben. But it didn't matter, because he made the anecdote so much more amusing.'

'It's extraordinary that you should say this to me now,' I answer, marvelling at the coincidence that I had only just been thinking and writing about the nature of truth, particularly in relation to Ben. 'What you have just told me seems to contradict the person I remember my father to be.' I then recount the conversation between Ben and Nigel on the documentary I had recently revisited. 'He seemed such a stickler for recalling things correctly,' I say. 'For being honest and truthful.'

Jeremy laughs heartily and is about to reply. 'Well, it...' he begins, turning his smiling face towards me, but the distraction of someone else's greeting interrupts him, and the moment has gone.

Ben reading by Rodrigo Moynihan, France, 1972

CODA

THE TRAIN JOURNEY THROUGH FRANCE TOOK MUCH LONGER in 1972 than it does now. To the girl it felt that they had been trapped in the stuffy carriage forever. They spent the final leg in silence, with the father reading and the daughter staring out of the window, and by the time they arrived at the rural station they were both limp with tiredness. The girl remained quiet as her father's artist friend drove them to his summer retreat. She sat in the back of the car and listened to him explaining who the current houseguests were: the widow of a novelist she had been studying at school, a historian from an American university, the painter's second wife and her adult son from her first marriage (both artists) plus the son's girlfriend. Finally the painter and his wife's own thirteen-year-old son.

The girl loved the house with its rambling rooms and a terrace where bowls of coffee and fresh croissants were consumed at breakfast under a flaking pergola. This was her favourite spot, a place to sit shaded from the fierceness of the August sun, happily writing letters to her friends and the boy she missed from school. The adult guests let her be and she had no interest in the sulky thirteen-year-old she hardly saw.

After breakfast everyone would disappear to occupy themselves as they wished – to read, write, paint, walk or swim. It was only at mealtimes that they came together to consume fish or meat and vegetables prepared by the housekeeper, washed down with carafes of local red wine and water held in terracotta jugs.

Halfway through the week it was the girl's sixteenth birthday. She wore a simple light blue cotton dress and the female guests weaved flowers into her long dark hair. The housekeeper produced a huge platter of lobsters for lunch which the girl did not touch for she had been disturbed by seeing them twitching in the kitchen earlier that morning. She felt shy, awkward, out of her depth, but the women noticed and were kind. Without fuss the housekeeper made her an omelette and the widow diverted everyone's attention by suggesting they play games as soon as lunch was over.

They grouped themselves into twos and threes for the first game. The birthday girl was paired with her father. Each group was to act out a situation in which something was to be subtly revealed without it being spelt out, and the others were to guess what this was. The pair who intrigued the audience for the longest time would win.

As the girl watched the various performances she felt increasingly jittery. They were all so witty and clever. Imaginary secrets, confessions, revelations were bandied around the table to bursts of laughter and interjections.

Their turn came last. The father gave his daughter an encouraging look.

'A kind of Truth Game?' he whispered.

'I know...' she whispered back, feeling energised. He leaned in as she continued, 'Pretend you're a prejudiced, horrible father, and I'm trying to tell you that my boyfriend is black.'

Her father grinned conspiratorially.

'So, Vanessa,' he said loudly and mock-pompously, 'when am I going to meet this young man of yours?'

'Well,' she squirmed, theatrically. 'I'm not sure you will like him...'

'Why ever not?'

'You may not think he is right for me...'

'Why, is he lazy?'

'Not at all, he is very hard working, ambitious, clever... and you should read the poetry he writes!'

'Is it good?'

'It's brilliant!'

'Does he treat you well?'

'Oh yes, he loves me very much.'

'Is he unreliable?'

'No, he's... um, very loyal,' she stammered slightly.

'And is he handsome?'

'Well... yes, he is tall and has beautiful dark eyes...'

And so it went on, and they got into their stride, and Vanessa channelled her nerves and shyness into *acting* shy and hesitant until she began enjoying the game and the attention, teasing the audience's expectations and presumptions. It took so long for them to get the 'truth', that they declared father and daughter were the winners.

'You should be an actress,' clapped the widow, 'you were so completely believable!'

And Vanessa's eyes shone, and she didn't bother to tell them that the boy from school she was in love with actually *was* black. She hadn't yet revealed his existence to her father. There would be time for that.

ACKNOWLEDGEMENTS

I would like to thank the following:

My agent Andrew Lownie.

Naim Attallah, David Elliott, James Pulford and Grace Pilkington at Quartet for getting this book on the road.

The friends who listened, read, encouraged and supported me.

Andrew and Ellie for helping me in more ways than I can possibly list here.

The characters in these stories, for inspiring me.

NOTES

1 Keith Vaughan, *Journal & Drawings, 1939-1965*, Alan Ross, 1966.
2 Vanessa Nicolson, *Have You Been Good?* Granta Books, 2015.
3 Graham Swift, *Mothering Sunday*, Simon & Schuster, 2016.
4 Excerpts from Ben Nicolson's journals courtesy of the Paul Mellon Centre, London.
5 Michael Bloch, *Jeremy Thorpe*, Little, Brown, 2015.
6 My grandmother Vita Sackville-West writing in September 1920, in Nigel Nicolson, *Portrait of a Marriage*, Weidenfeld & Nicolson, 1973.
7 Since writing this the law has been changed to allow civil partnerships in Italy, the very last Western European country to do so. However, same-sex couples have still not been granted the right to adopt their partners' biological children.

LIST OF ILLUSTRATIONS

Vanessa as a teenager with her father Ben Nicolson, 1973.

Inconstancy, 1303–1305, by Giotto. Detail from the cycle of frescoes *The Vices and Virtues*, Scrovegni Chapel, Padua, Italy. De Agostini Picture Library / A. Dagli Orti / Bridgeman Images.

Wrath, 1303–1305, by Giotto. Detail from the cycle of frescoes *The Vices and Virtues*, Scrovegni Chapel, Padua, Italy. Mondadori Portfolio / Archivio Antonio Quattrone / Antonio Quattrone / Bridgeman Images.

Envy, 1303–1305, by Giotto. Detail from the cycle of frescoes *The Vices and Virtues*, Scrovegni Chapel, Padua, Italy. De Agostini Picture Library / A. Dagli Orti / Bridgeman Images.

Untitled cartoon, 1950, by Michael Rutherston, detail.

Martyrdom of St Sebastian, ca 1473, by Sandro Botticelli. De Agostini Picture Library / Bridgeman Images.

Mrs William Morris in a Blue Silk Dress, 1868, by Dante Gabriel Rossetti. Kelmscott Manor, Oxfordshire, UK / Bridgeman Images.

Kate's Madness, 1806–1807, by Henry Fuseli. De Agostini Picture Library / Bridgeman Images.

Ben reading, 1972, by Rodrigo Moynihan. Red chalk, signed and dated '11.VIII. '72' with dedication 'To Vanessa'.